# THE SHRIKE
## ACTING EDITION

BY JOSEPH KRAMM

DRAMATISTS
PLAY SERVICE
INC.

# THE SHRIKE
Copyrights © Renewed 1977, 1980, Joseph Kramm
Copyright ©1952, Joseph Kramm
Copyright ©1950, Joseph Kramm
as an unpublished work

### All Rights Reserved

CAUTION: Professionals and amateurs are hereby warned that performance of THE SHRIKE is subject to a royalty. It is fully protected under the copyright laws of the United States of America, and of all countries covered by the International Copyright Union (including the Dominion of Canada and the rest of the British Commonwealth), and of all countries covered by the Pan-American Copyright Convention, the Universal Copyright Convention, the Berne Convention, and of all countries with which the United States has reciprocal copyright relations. All rights, including professional/amateur stage rights, motion picture, recitation, lecturing, public reading, radio broadcasting, television, video or sound recording, all other forms of mechanical or electronic reproduction, such as CD-ROM, CD-I, information storage and retrieval systems and photocopying, and the rights of translation into foreign languages, are strictly reserved. Particular emphasis is laid upon the matter of readings, permission for which must be secured from the Author's agent in writing.

The amateur stage performance rights in THE SHRIKE are controlled exclusively by the DRAMATISTS PLAY SERVICE, INC., 440 Park Avenue South, New York, N.Y. 10016. No non-professional performance of the Play may be given without obtaining in advance the written permission of the DRAMATISTS PLAY SERVICE, INC., and paying the requisite fee.

Inquiries concerning all other rights should be addressed to Dramatists Play Service, Inc., 440 Park Avenue South, New York, N.Y. 10016.

### SPECIAL NOTE
Anyone receiving permission to produce THE SHRIKE is required to give credit to the Author as sole and exclusive Author of the Play on the title page of all programs distributed in connection with performances of the Play and in all instances in which the title of the Play appears for purposes of advertising, publicizing or otherwise exploiting the Play and/or a production thereof. The name of the Author must appear on a separate line, in which no other name appears, immediately beneath the title and in size of type equal to 50% of the largest, most prominent letter used for the title of the Play. No person, firm or entity may receive credit larger or more prominent than that accorded the Author.

THE SHRIKE was first presented by Jose Ferrer at the Cort Theater, New York City, on January 15, 1952. Milton Baron was associate producer, and the setting was by Howard Bay. The play was directed by Mr. Ferrer. The cast was as follows:

| | |
|---|---|
| MISS CARDELL | Phyllis Hill |
| FLEMING | Tom Reynolds |
| MISS HANSEN | Jeannette Dowling |
| DR. KRAMER | Stephen Elliott |
| PERKINS | James Hawthorne Bey |
| GROSBERG | William Bush |
| DR. BARROW | Isabel Bonner |
| PATIENT | Vincent Donahue |
| ANN DOWNS | Judith Evelyn |
| JIM DOWNS | Jose Ferrer |
| DR. SCHLESINGER | Somer Alberg |
| DON GREGORY | Philip Huston |
| SAM TAGER | Will Lee |
| GEORGE O'BRIEN | Martin Newman |
| JOE MAJOR | Joe Comadore |
| JOHN ANKORITIS | Will Kuluva |
| FRANK CARLISLE | Leigh Whipper |
| WILLIAM SCHLOSS | Billy M. Greene |
| DR. BELLMAN | Kendall Clark |
| MISS WINGATE | Mary Bell |
| HARRY DOWNS | Edward Platt |
| TOM BLAIR | Arthur Jarrett |

All the action takes place in City Hospital

## SCENES

### ACT I

SCENE 1—11:30 in the morning—Tuesday.
SCENE 2—2:00 A.M.—the next morning—Wednesday.
SCENE 3—Noon—two days later—Friday.
SCENE 4—11:00 A.M.—three days later—Monday.
SCENE 5—Afternoon—immediately following.

## Act II

Scene 1—Just before lunch—the next day—Tuesday.
Scene 2—2:00 P.M.—the next day—Wednesday.
Scene 3—Close to 9:00 P.M.—the same day.
Scene 4—2:00 P.M.—the next day—Thursday.
Scene 5—3:00 P.M.—five days later—Tuesday.

## Act III

Scene 1—1:30 P.M.—two days later—Thursday.
Scene 2—Afternoon—four days later—Monday.
Scene 3—2:00 P.M.—three days later—Thursday.
Scene 4—10:00 A.M.—the next day—Friday.

## AUTHOR'S PRODUCTION NOTES

The windows and door constitute the set. There are no realistic walls. The windows can be suspended from the fly gallery, or ceiling, and fixed to the floor with wire or rope painted black. The bottom of the windows should be about five feet from the floor. They can be made proportionate to any stage, those in the New York production being six feet wide each, and twelve feet high. The door should be fairly heavy, about two to three inches thick, and three and a half feet wide; the height, the usual six feet nine inches.

Entrances right and left, other than the door, are from between the velour hangings, as indicated in the script, down right, or up left, etc.

The general color of the set and props is gray, somewhat lighter than what is known as battleship gray. The bevelling of the windows changes from gray at the bottom to black at the top. The door is gray; the beds, desks, chairs, metal cabinets, and hospital screen, are all gray. The velour hangings are, of course, black.

The lock in the door should be practical to the extent that the turning of the key should make a sound, but the tumbler or latch should be removed to avoid the possibility of its failure during performance and so make it impossible for anyone to enter or leave. The lock is on the downstage side of the door, and the door opens on-stage. The bell is located on the off-stage side of the door, and is practical. It is a mechanical bell, of the sort that rings with a twist of a handle on the bell itself, and each actor using the bell works it himself on cue.

The Schlesinger and Bellman scenes, Act I, Scene 4, and Act II, Scene 2, are simple to set up. The hospital screen, which was used in the first scene in front of Jim's bed, is extended its full width, which, if each panel is three feet wide, should be nine feet. It would be wise to make some provision to keep the screen rigid during these scenes so that either side panel will not move during the playing of the scene. This can be simply done by placing a thin iron or wooden rod through the panels, and it is best done between scenes one and two in the first act, when the screen is removed from Jim's bed and can be brought off-stage for this purpose. It should be brought back on stage for the third scene, and there it remains (consult diagram) for the entire play, except for the Schlesinger and Bellman scenes. The screen, for these scenes, is placed directly center stage, in front of the beds. Kramer's desk is placed in front of it, and centered, and the two chairs are placed as indicated in the body of the script. That's all there is to it. With two or three spotlights providing their concentrated light on this area, there will, of course, be some spill of light on the beds in the background. This doesn't matter—it didn't in New York—and you will save time and energy by not trying to conceal the background.

Apart from whatever general and specific lighting you may have, you should provide five or six hanging fixtures for the stage. These are simple fixtures, of the sort with a wide, inverted, shallow bowl, for the reflection and shade. They are hung in a line across the downstage area, parallel to the footlights, the first one hanging over Hansen's desk; the second, over Kramer's desk, and the others spaced across the stage. In the night scenes, only those fixtures over the specific desk areas indicated should be on, supplementing the general lighting and providing the motivation for light. In Act II, Scene 3, for example, when Miss Wingate turns out the lights, the fixture over her desk should remain on, with the appropriate covering shots, of course.

*Keys:* All the actors using a key to open and lock the door should be provided with a ring containing a number of keys, and a chain or cord so that one end can be attached to a belt or other part of their clothing.

*Trolley:* This trolley or carriage, on which Jim Downs is wheeled in, is of the sort familiarly seen in hospitals for the transportation of patients from ward to ward, or ward to operating room, etc.

*Sphygmomanometer:* A blood-pressure instrument. The actor playing Kramer should get a doctor friend to show him how to use it, so that it looks professional on stage.

When Miss Cardell enters with Perkins carrying the stand and bottle for the intravenous injection, she waits for Perkins to leave, then places the kidney-shaped tray on the chair left of Jim's bed. She wipes Jim's arm with a piece of cotton, supposedly soaked with alcohol, then takes needle from tray, fixes it in the loose end of the rubber tube hanging from the inverted bottle, and, ostensibly, injects the needle into Jim's arm. She can conceal this by placing the needle under the sleeve of Jim's hospital gown, and covering the arm with his blanket.

The making of the bed by Grosberg and Perkins, before Jim is wheeled in, can be difficult and complicated unless the proper preparation is made in advance. The bottom sheet should be so folded that Grosberg and Perkins, when they take up their respective ends, should be able to open the sheet to its full length with one motion. They should then proceed to tuck in the ends first, and make the hospital corners as required. If the bed is not completely made before Perkins must go to the door (and it probably won't be), this business can be completed by Barrow and Perkins after Jim has been placed in the bed—covering him with the blanket, etc.

The food on the trays should be edible. Each tray contains a coffee cup, a cereal bowl, and a spoon. Apple sauce in the bowl will usually be best, since it won't dry the throat.

*Extras, orderly, attendants, and visitors:*

The *orderly* who pushes Jim in on the trolley in the first scene does two other jobs. He is one of the attendants who drags O'Brien off in the second act, and with a change of costume, he is one of the patients in the waiting group in Act III, Scene 3.

The *patient* in the first act, "the silent one," is also one of the attendants who drags O'Brien off, and one of the patients in the waiting group in Act III.

The *woman visitor*, "Ankoritis' wife," can be Miss Hansen, in civilian clothes, with a shawl over her head. If it is possible, it is best of course, to have a Negro girl as Major's visitor. If not, it can be either a man or woman, white or Negro. Also, if it is possible, it helps the appearance of the scene, if two more extras can be used as patients in the waiting group in Act III.

The *calypso songs* Major sings in Act II, Scene 5, can be "Ugly Woman" and "Matilda." These are the songs used in the New York production. "Ugly Woman" is used for the beginning of the scene; "Matilda," for the end.

*Costumes:* All pajamas are of the cheap, striped, washed-out, faded, cotton flannel variety.

1. Patient: Pajamas.
2. Fleming: Pajamas.
3. Miss Hansen: Graduate nurse's all-white uniform.
4. Dr. Kramer: Dark trousers (his own), white shirt, tie, and white, lapelled doctor's coat.
5. Grosberg: His own trousers, shirt, and tie.
6. Perkins: Army sun-tan shirt and trousers, and civilian tie.
7. Jim: *First act:* Pajama trousers, hospital examination gown (the kind that ties in the back).
   *Second act:* Pajamas, top and bottom.
   *Third act:* His own trousers, army sun-tan shirt, shoes without laces.
8. Orderly: His own trousers, shirt, and tie, and white lapelled, hospital coat. As the attendant, he wears the same thing. As a patient in the third act, he wears his own trousers, and shirt. Of course, no tie. No patient wears a tie, at any time.
9. Ann: Her own clothes, not too stylish, but in good taste, and with as few changes as her vanity will permit—two or three will suffice.

10. Miss Cardell: Student nurse's uniform.
11. Dr. Barrow: Her own clothes, with a three-quarter length, lapelled, white doctor's coat.
12. O'Brien: *Act II—Scene 1*: His own shirt and trousers, shoes without laces.
    *Scene 3*: Pajamas.
13. Tager: *Act II, Scene 1*: His own trousers, and pajama top.
    *Scene 3*: Pajamas.
    *Scene 5*, and thereafter, same as Scene 1.
14. Schloss: *Act II—Scene 1*: His own shirt and trousers.
    *Scene 3*: Pajamas.
    *Scene 5*, and thereafter: Same as Scene 1.
15. Ankoritis: Pajamas, throughout.
16. Major: Pajamas, throughout.
17. Carlisle: Pajamas, throughout.
18. Gregory: Army sun-tan shirt and trousers, with civilian tie.
19. Miss Wingate: Graduate nurse's all-white uniform.
20. Dr. Bellman: His own clothes, throughout—*no white coat at any time.*
21. Harry Downs: His own clothes, including overcoat.
22. Tom Blair: His own clothes, including overcoat.

*Playing notes for non-professionals:*

A few words only to indicate the playing key of a few important scenes. In the Schlesinger scene, Jim must become aware after the first few moments that it is not going to be as easy to get out as he imagined. From that point on, a fear overcomes him—all the more disturbing because it is intangible. He doesn't know what to be afraid of, because he is given no clue by Schlesinger, but he realizes as he goes on that he is faced with a formidable obstacle to his release. This, coupled with the natural anxiety to go home, creates the tension that leads Jim to explode and resist with strength all the questions about Charlotte. And, of course, it is this very explosion that causes Schlesinger to give credence to all that Ann has insinuated against Jim.

In the first Bellman scene, Jim is resentful and antagonistic. His action, throughout the play, is to get out of the hospital, but in this scene, the action is colored by the emotional experience of the previous scene, and the desire to assert himself. This motivates the resentment and antagonism.

In the scene with Ann, in the second act, Jim is suspicious but getting more and more desperate, so that he is forced to accept Ann's help against his will.

The first scene of the third act finds Jim cynical and mistrustful, which provides the soil for the seed of his brother's advice. He makes his choice, which is a violation of himself. In the second and third scenes of this act, he walks a tight rope, allowing only a momentary outburst against Barrow and Bellman in the second scene when he tries to recover from the trap into which he fell with one of his answers. The last scene with Bellman finds Jim on a thin wire, sparring for his life. When he finishes the telephone conversation with Ann, and breaks into sobs, it is the realization that having made the choice of the lesser of two evils he has simply exchanged one evil for another, that motivates this reaction.

# THE SHRIKE

## ACT I

### SCENE 1

SCENE: *Ward MN3, City Hospital.*

*Up* R., *extending two-thirds of the way across the back of stage, are four windows. These are tall, not too narrow, and close together. The window itself is set in a bevelled frame of ten to twelve inches in depth. Heavy wire screens cover front of each window frame.*

*Down* L. *a door. This is a heavy door, set in a substantial frame, and angled on-stage from down* L. *corner. Above door, set in the same frame, is a wire screen, through which we see the light of the outside corridor.*

*This is the only door to this ward, to this floor, as a matter of fact, from any other part of the building—and it is constantly locked. Nurses, attendants, and doctors who use it must use a key to get in or out.*

*Down* L., *near door, is a small desk. Behind desk, a chair. The charge nurse,* MISS HANSEN, *a middle-aged woman who has been soured rather than mellowed by her contact with illness, is seated at this desk. She is making notes on some of the charts. There is a phone on this desk, and a goose-neck desk lamp.*

*A few feet to* R. *of* MISS HANSEN'S *desk is another small desk, with two chairs, one on either side.* DR. KRAMER, *a tall, good-looking man in his late thirties, is sitting at this desk, reading a chart.*

*When the curtain rises, we see only two beds in the ward. These are placed in front of the windows, extending down-*

stage. Bed No. 1 is on R. Bed No. 3 is approximately in C. stage. There is space between these beds for another bed to be moved in when it is called for. To L. of beds No. 1 and No. 3, placed near head of each bed, is a small metal cabinet for the patient's belongings. On cabinet next to bed No. 1 is another goose-neck desk lamp. In bed No. 1 we see "the silent one." When he is awake he is sitting up in his bed staring quietly into space. In bed No. 3 we find FLEMING.

TIME: 11:30 *in the morning, Tuesday.*

*There is silence for a brief moment.* DR. KRAMER *and* MISS HANSEN *are busy with their respective tasks.* FLEMING *is smoking a cigarette. He knows this is against the rules so the cigarette is held cupped in his hand and the smoke he doesn't swallow is waved surreptitiously away.*

*When he has taken one or two puffs,* MISS CARDELL *enters* R. *She carries* FLEMING'S *chart in her hand. As she enters,* FLEMING *quickly crushes cigarette out against side of his metal cabinet.* MISS CARDELL *stops briefly when she sees this.*

MISS CARDELL. You were smoking, Mr. Fleming. (*She continues to* FLEMING'S *bed, hangs chart at foot of it on hook provided for it.*)
FLEMING. (*A man of about fifty.*) No, I wasn't.
MISS CARDELL. A man with a heart condition like yours—honestly! (*She goes to up* R. *of* FLEMING'S *bed.*) Give me the cigarettes, Mr. Fleming.
FLEMING. I haven't got any cigarettes.
MISS CARDELL. (R. *of* FLEMING: *lifts blankets.*) I don't have all day—now give me the ——
FLEMING. Look in the cabinet, if you don't believe me.
MISS CARDELL. Do you want me to call an attendant, Mr. Fleming? (*He subsides.*) Then let me have the cigarettes.
FLEMING. (*Pulls blanket back—irritably.*) All right. (*Reaching under mattress at head of bed.*) Here.
MISS CARDELL. (*Puts cigarettes in her pocket.*) I'll have to report it—you know that —— Where are the matches? (*Phone rings at* MISS HANSEN'S *desk.*)
MISS HANSEN. MN3—Miss Hansen.
FLEMING. Here. (*From pocket of his pajamas.*)

MISS CARDELL. (*Moves around to* L. *of bed, tucking in blanket as she goes.*) Where did you get them?
MISS HANSEN. Right away. (*Hangs up.*) Emergency suicide coming up, Dr. Kramer.
KRAMER. (*Without looking up.*) Is there a bed?
MISS HANSEN. Miss Cardell, is there a vacant bed?
MISS CARDELL. (*Turns to* MISS HANSEN.) Not in this ward. (*A few steps down to* MISS HANSEN.) Mr. Fleming has been smoking, Miss Hansen.
MISS HANSEN. (*Paying no attention.*) Hm-hmmm. (MISS CARDELL *looks briefly at* MISS HANSEN, *turns helplessly back to* FLEMING. *She goes to* U. L. *of* FLEMING'S *bed.*)
KRAMER. And call Dr. Barrow, Miss Hansen.
MISS HANSEN. Yes, Dr. Kramer. (*On phone.*) Dr. Barrow, please. Dr. Kramer, MN3. Emergency suicide. (GROSBERG *appears from* D. R. *pushing empty wheel chair.* MISS HANSEN *sees him.*) Oh, Mr. Grosberg, will you and Mr. Perkins bring a bed to 3? Emergency.
GROSBERG. (*Shrugs shoulders.*) I don't know where we'll find one unless somebody dies. (*Turns wheel chair around, goes off* R.)
MISS CARDELL. (*As she starts to exit* D. R., *crossing in front of* FLEMING'S *bed.*) That doesn't make any difference. You know the kind of patients we have here! (*Stops, looks back at* FLEMING.) Suppose one of them took those matches while you were asleep and set fire to something?
FLEMING. You're right. I'm sorry.
MISS CARDELL. (*As she goes out* D. R.) I should think for your own good—Honestly!
MISS HANSEN. (*Hangs up phone, to* KRAMER.) Dr. Barrow will be up as soon as she can.
KRAMER. Thank you. (PERKINS *and* GROSBERG *enter* R., *wheel in a bed in time to hear* MISS HANSEN'S *announcement to* KRAMER. PERKINS, *a Negro, backs in, holding head of bed.* GROSBERG *is at foot. There is a blanket, folded linen, and a pillow on bed. They roll bed to just L. of bed No. 1, leave it downstage.* GROSBERG *takes blanket and pillow, places them on foot of bed No. 1, and he and* PERKINS *begin immediately to make bed. They speak as they work.*)
GROSBERG. Dr. Barrow's nice. You know her? She's a psychiatrist. You ever been psyched?
PERKINS. Uh-uh.

MISS HANSEN. Oh, Grosberg, leave it right there for now. We can move it later.
GROSBERG. (*As they make bed.*) I have a friend who's being psyched. He says it's wonderful. The things you say about yourself.
FLEMING. Hssst, Grosberg!
GROSBERG. He goes three times a week and he can't wait for the next session.
FLEMING. Hssst!
GROSBERG. (*Going R. to* FLEMING.) Can't you see I'm busy? There's an emergency coming up—a suicide. (*Crosses* U. R. *to* FLEMING. FLEMING *gives him dollar bill. As* GROSBERG *pockets it, he goes back to making bed.* PERKINS *has gone to foot of bed.* GROSBERG *goes to head.*)
FLEMING. (*Whispers.*) Chesterfields.
GROSBERG. (*Finishes making bed with* PERKINS.) Now why would a man want to do that? Some woman, I guess. It's always a woman. (*Bell rings.*) There it is. We'd better hurry. (PERKINS *and* GROSBERG *roll bed into position between beds No. 1 and No. 3. At same time* MISS HANSEN *starts for door. Takes key from pocket, opens door.* PERKINS *crosses to* R. *of* MISS HANSEN.)
MISS HANSEN. (*To* ATTENDANT *standing in corridor behind trolley, on which is lying* JIM DOWNS, *covered from neck down with a hospital sheet.*) The suicide? (PERKINS, *on* MISS HANSEN'S *line, moves quickly to foot of trolley. He helps draw it down.*)
ATTENDANT. (*As he pushes trolley in.*) Yeah. Here's his card.
MISS HANSEN. (*Takes card.*) This way. (ATTENDANT *and* PERKINS *roll trolley to* C., *just* R. *of* KRAMER'S *desk.* KRAMER *puts chart down as soon as door is opened. He takes sphygmomanometer from drawer in his desk, hangs stethoscope, which was in pocket of his white jacket, on his neck, and crosses to* R. *of his desk, awaiting trolley.* MISS HANSEN, *through foregoing business, the instant trolley clears her, steps in front of* ANN, *blocking her way as she enters behind* ATTENDANT.) Who are you?
ANN. His wife.
MISS HANSEN. This way. (HANSEN *motions with her head in direction of trolley.* ANN *goes quickly to within two or three feet of trolley.* ATTENDANT *leaves trolley immediately it is in position, crosses* L., *exits through door.* HANSEN *locks door after him, puts* JIM'S *card on her desk, joins group around trolley.* KRAMER, *the moment trolley reaches him, turns back sheet on upstage side, ties rubber pipe on* JIM'S *arm, takes his blood pressure.* DR. BARROW *enters from* D. R. *during blood*

*pressure business.' She goes downstage of trolley, close to* KRAMER. *The group, when it is complete, looks like this:*

PERKINS

GROSBERG    KRAMER  HANSEN

Trolley    ANN

BARROW

KRAMER. (*When he has finished, looks at* BARROW.) 110 over 60. (*Removes blood pressure instrument quickly, hands it to* HANSEN, *who puts it on his desk. Slaps patient's face several times.*) Wake up! Wake up! (*Looks to* ANN.) What's his name?
ANN. Jim.
KRAMER. (*Slapping his face hard.*) Jim! Wake up, Jim! (*A low grunt from* JIM.) That's it! Wake up!
BARROW. (*Leans over* JIM, *talking as to a deaf person.*) What did you take? (*Another grunt from* JIM.)
ANN. Phenobarbital.
KRAMER. Let *him* answer.
ANN. I'm sorry.
KRAMER. (*Shaking* JIM.) What did you take?
JIM. (*Thickly, through a haze.*) Phen-o-bar-bital.
BARROW. What?
KRAMER. Speak up, Jim! Again! What did you take?
JIM. (*No clearer than before.*) Phen-o-bar-bital.
KRAMER. When? (*No answer. Slaps him again.*) Come on, Jim! Wake up! When did you take it? (*No answer.*) How many did you take?
JIM. (*Slowly, thickly—it should not be understood by audience.*) A hun-dred and fif-ty six.
KRAMER. What? (*He looks at* BARROW.)
BARROW. That's impossible.
KRAMER. You ask him again.
BARROW. (*Leans over him again.*) Jim! Wake up, Jim! (*She shakes him.*) How many pills did you take?
JIM. (*Same as before.*) A hun-dred and fif-ty six.
BARROW. (*Her hand on his face.*) He's so cold.
ANN. He was lying on the floor. It was an unheated apartment.
BARROW. That may have saved him. If the place had been warm, it would be all over.

KRAMER. *When* did he take them—that's more important!
BARROW. Jim! Try to tell me, Jim! When did you take the pills? (*No answer.*)
KRAMER. (*Calmly*—*to* PERKINS *and* GROSBERG.) Move him to the bed. Miss Hansen, order a saline solution with high vitamin content for intravenous injection. Perkins, screen the bed. Grosberg, get a stomach pump. (HANSEN *goes at once to her desk and phones.* PERKINS *and* GROSBERG *roll trolley to between beds* No. 2 *and* No. 3. BARROW *goes to* U. R. *of* JIM'S *bed.* PERKINS *and* GROSBERG, *at* JIM'S *head and feet, lift him from trolley and place him in bed.* GROSBERG *goes out at once off* R. BARROW *and* PERKINS *complete the action, covering him with blanket, and fixing pillow.* PERKINS *then goes quickly for the 3-fold hospital screen, which has been standing, folded, and placed at an angle offstage, close to bed* No. 1. *He opens screen and places it in front of* JIM'S *bed, fixing side panels so that people will not have too much difficulty going to, or leaving* JIM'S *bed.* BARROW *remains with* JIM. PERKINS *goes off* R. *when screen is in place. Though speed is essential in all this business, the activity must look efficient, not rushed, as though everyone knew his job perfectly.* KRAMER *and* ANN *watch only for a few seconds, then* KRAMER *turns to* ANN. KRAMER, *to* ANN.) We can't tell yet. He'll be on the critical list for a while, so you can stay here if you like. (KRAMER *goes to* ANN, *takes her arm, indicates chair* L. *of his desk.* ANN *sits. As he goes back to his own chair.*) Miss Hansen, I want special nurses for at least forty-eight hours. (*He sits.*)
MISS HANSEN. I'm not sure we can get them. This is Thanksgiving week—most of them will be away.
KRAMER. We must have them.
MISS HANSEN. What about her? Can she afford special nurses?
ANN. (*Turns to* HANSEN.) I'll manage. (*Turns back to* KRAMER.) Please get them. Get anything that's needed. (MISS HANSEN *picks up phone to call—her voice in ad lib undertone.*)
KRAMER. Now, how did this happen?
ANN. I don't really know. I got a phone call from his brother at about 9:30 this morning ——
KRAMER. (*Puzzled.*) Wait a minute—weren't you there? I thought you were his wife?
ANN. I am. We were separated. He was living in this cold-water flat.
KRAMER. I see.
ANN. His brother's a businessman in a small town near Pittsburgh. When he called me—it's a funny thing, I couldn't sleep all night. I

knew something had happened to Jim—his brother said he just received a letter from Jim saying he was going to take the pills. He told me to get over there as quickly as possible, and of course I did. (*Fighting against tears.*) I called the police —— (*The tears give way.*) I'm sorry, doctor—I'm not a hysterical woman.
KRAMER. That's all right. You've been fine.
ANN. I called the police and told them what happened. (MISS CARDELL and PERKINS *enter from* R. PERKINS *first, carrying stand and bottle containing saline solution.* CARDELL *follows directly behind him carrying a kidney-shaped sterilizing pan.* PERKINS *places stand to* L. *of* JIM'S *bed, near his head, and goes off* R. CARDELL *fixes needle in* JIM'S *arm, then also leaves* R. *This business takes place behind screen.* ANN *is distracted by this activity and half rises out of her chair to watch, though she doesn't stop talking.* KRAMER *leans across desk to place his hand on her arm, and* ANN *sits down again, still telling her story.*) I gave them the address and thank God they were there by the time I arrived. They tried to break the door, but the lock held, and one of them went up to the roof, came down the fire-escape and climbed in through the window. He let us in. My husband was on the floor in the living-room.
KRAMER. What did the police do?
ANN. They shook him and slapped him, the way you did—and they asked him what he took.
KRAMER. Was he able to tell them?
ANN. Yes. He said phenobarbital, the way he told you.
KRAMER. This happened about an hour ago, I take it?
ANN. When we found him?
KRAMER. Yes.
ANN. Just about.
KRAMER. We've *got* to find out when he took the pills. Do you have any idea at all, Mrs. ——?
ANN. Downs. Well, let me see—this is Tuesday, Tuesday. I talked with him on the phone at about 12:30 Sunday night. (MISS CARDELL *exits* R.)
KRAMER. And not since?
ANN. No. We made an appointment to see each other at four o'clock Monday afternoon—that was yesterday—at my place. He didn't show up. That's the last I knew until his brother called me this morning.
KRAMER. (*Has been making notes on chart for* JIM, *which he got from his desk. He now stops to write briefly.*) Well—we'll see ——
ANN. (*As he writes.*) Oh—the—eh—the postmark on the letter?
KRAMER. (*Looks up.*) What letter?

ANN. The one that ——
BARROW. (*Comes from behind screen to* R. *of* KRAMER'S *desk—addresses* ANN.) Excuse me—are you Charlotte?
KRAMER. (*To* BARROW.) This is his wife. (*To* ANN.) Dr. Barrow's a psychiatrist.
BARROW. What's your name?
ANN. Ann.
BARROW. I wanted to identify the name Charlotte.
ANN. She's just someone he knew.
BARROW. I see. (*She looks at* ANN *briefly, returns to* JIM.)
KRAMER. You were speaking about a postmark on a letter?
ANN. Yes—the one he sent to his brother. There'd be a New York postmark on it—you might be able to tell approximately from that. I can call him on the phone.
MISS HANSEN. What is his religion, Mrs. Downs?
ANN. (*Turns to* HANSEN.) Protestant.
MISS HANSEN. Any special sect?
ANN. He wasn't a regular church-goer—why?
MISS HANSEN. I'll have to call the minister. It's a hospital rule. (*Turns back, picks up phone.*)
ANN. (*To* KRAMER, *again fighting for control.*) It's as bad as that?
KRAMER. It's just a precaution. I'd call his brother, if I were you, Mrs. Downs.
ANN. But ——
KRAMER. It's all right. Why don't you call him now? The phone is downstairs.
ANN. I want to be here when ——
KRAMER. You have no idea how many men have walked out of here after last rites have been said over them.
ANN. (*Rises.*) You're sure it's all right?
KRAMER. Yes. Make your call. (*As he crosses to door, and taking key from his pocket.*) Everything is being done for him that can possibly be done.
ANN. Thank you, doctor. (*Starts* L., *then turns* L. *of desk.*) May I see him—for just a moment?
KRAMER. All right. (*She crosses* R., *goes behind screen. A brief pause, then quietly.*)
ANN. Jim! Jim! (*After a moment, she appears, starts for door.*)

LIGHTS FADE QUICKLY

# ACT I

## Scene 2

SCENE: *The same.*

TIME: *About 2 A.M. next morning—Wednesday.*

*The ward is dark.*

*The screen in front of* JIM'S *bed has been returned to its original position at beginning of Scene 1. A chair has been placed near* JIM'S *bed, on* L. *side, near his head. Saline bottle and stand are still present.*

ANN *is sitting in* KRAMER'S *chair. She is trying hard to keep awake.* MISS CARDELL *comes from* JIM'S *bed with thermometer in her hand. She goes to* MISS HANSEN'S *desk, records temperature.*

FLEMING *and* PATIENT *are asleep in their beds.*

MISS CARDELL. (*As she crosses to her desk from* JIM'S *bed.*) You ought to go home, Mrs. Downs.
ANN. I'd rather stay, if it's all right. At least *here* I know what's happening.
MISS CARDELL. But it's nearly two A.M. You ought to get some rest.
ANN. I'm all right. If only I could get a cup of coffee.
MISS CARDELL. You'll find some in the kitchen—down the hall. (ANN *starts to get up,* MISS CARDELL *looks up at her.*) Never mind—I'll get it for you.
ANN. Thank you.
MISS CARDELL. (*Rises.*) You've been wonderful, I'll say that for you. (*As she crosses to* R.) Also, you're crazy—no man is worth it.
BARROW. (*Enters* D. R., *goes to* MISS CARDELL *as she meets her near entrance.*) Mrs. Downs still here? (MISS CARDELL *nods to desk, leaves* R. BARROW *crosses to* R. *side of* JIM'S *bed. To* ANN, *as she goes to* JIM.) How do you feel? (ANN *nods.* BARROW *checks* JIM'S *pulse.*) You've been a big help, but you must have some reserve. (*Crosses to foot of bed, looks at chart.*)
ANN. How does it look, Dr. Barrow?
BARROW. It's more on the good side, I think I can say. You've **been** with him all day?

17

ANN. I haven't left him for a moment.
BARROW. (*Replaces chart, crosses to* R. *of* ANN.) Has he spoken yet?
ANN. A few things.
BARROW. What?
ANN. Why didn't you let me die, he said. Why didn't you let me die? He repeated it several times. I wanted to question him, but I didn't think I should.
BARROW. Oh, by all means—that's most important. When he starts talking again, you must try to keep him awake.
ANN. I'm afraid to do something wrong.
BARRROW. Not at all. (*As she crosses in front of* ANN *to* L. *of* KRAMER'S *desk.*) You must question him, talk to him—get all the information you can. The things he says now are the most important. (*Turns to* ANN *when she is there.*) That's what he really thinks and feels. As he regains consciousness, he will begin to build the walls again. You understand? (BARROW *sits chair* L. *of* KRAMER'S *desk.*)
ANN. Hm-hmm.
BARROW. (*Taking cigarettes from her pocket.*) Cigarette?
ANN. No—thank you.
BARROW. Self-deception. His defenses will come back to protect him. (*Lights cigarette.*)
ANN. I understand.
BARROW. You spoke to his brother this morning?
ANN. Yes.
BARROW. Was there anything in the letter—any reason for taking his life?
ANN. I don't think so. His brother read the letter to me on the phone, I don't remember anything.
BARROW. Have you any idea why Jim didn't leave a letter for *you*, Mrs. Downs?
ANN. No—unless he felt—I don't know. (MISS CARDELL *enters* R., *crosses to* ANN *with coffee.* ANN *looks up.*) Oh, thank you, Miss Cardell, you're very kind.
MISS CARDELL. Not at all.
BARROW. Coffee! I'd love some —— (*A questioning look at* MISS CARDELL.) Would it be too much trouble?
MISS CARDELL. (*Doesn't like to run errands for doctors.*) Not at all. (*Crosses* R., *exits.*)
BARROW. What does your husband do?
ANN. He's in the theater.

BARROW. Singing—dancing?
ANN. No—what they call the legitimate theater—he's a director.
BARROW. Has he worked recently?
ANN. No. Several years ago he directed a show that got good notices. . . .
BARROW. On Broadway?
ANN. Yes. The critics said he was a fine new talent.
BARROW. Then I don't understand ——?
ANN. Well, that's the theater. It ended right there. He expected to be flooded with offers from other producers, the movies, what not—but nothing came of it. Time went by—several years now, in fact—the show was forgotten. He never got another job.
BARROW. I see. Is there anything more?
ANN. He had to start all over again—anything at all, just to make a living —— It made him very unhappy. (JIM *moans.* ANN *turns to him.*) That's Jim—he's trying to move. (*Turns back to* BARROW.) Once he said—why did they tie my hands and feet?
BARROW. You understand—we *had* to tie them—the intravenous needle in his arm. (*Another moan.*) Maybe he's awake. (BARROW *rises first, crosses to* R. *of* JIM'S *bed.* ANN *rises a second later, crosses to* L. *of* JIM'S *bed.* BARROW *turns on goose-neck lamp on cabinet* L. *of silent patient's bed.*) What's the matter, Jim?
JIM. (*Still indistinct—in everything he says there is a sense of struggle.*) Why don't you let me die?
BARROW. Why do you want to die, Jim?
JIM. I'm no good. (*Loud.*) No good!
FLEMING. (*Sits up in bed.*) What the hell is he yelling about?
BARROW. Quiet, Mr. Fleming.
FLEMING. (*Lies down again.*) Christ—try to sleep ——
ANN. He *is* very loud.
BARROW. He's fighting. (*She leans over* JIM'S *bed.*) Jim, why do you say you're no good?
JIM. Nowhere, after all these years ——
ANN. (*Bending over* JIM.) There's still time, dear—you'll be all right.
JIM. I had my chance—I didn't make it ——
ANN. You will. . . .
JIM. There's no time any more.—I'm an old man.
ANN. (*Sits in chair* L. *of* JIM'S *bed.*) You're not, Jim. I told you so many times ——
BARROW. (*To* ANN—*quietly.*) How old is he?
ANN. Forty-two.

BARROW. But that's young.
ANN. I know—but he's had that idea for several years. He insists he's an old man.
BARROW. Why do you think you're an old man, Jim?
JIM. Why?
BARROW. Yes—why do you think you're an old man?
JIM. Why don't you let me die? I'll only have to do it again.
ANN. No, dear—things will be different ——
BARROW. You're a young man, Jim—there's time to change.
JIM. Don't tell me that —— (*Suddenly yells.*) Why am I tied?
ANN. (*Quietly.*) Jim!
JIM. What?
ANN. I love you. I love you. Do you hear me, Jim?
JIM. It's too late, Ann, I don't want you to love me. (ANN *rises, takes a few steps downstage. Then, more subdued—mumbled, so as not to be understood by the audience.*) A hundred and fifty-six pills ——
BARROW. Of course, *that* I can hardly believe.
ANN. He's said it several times. (ANN *goes to* R. *of* KRAMER'S *desk again.*)
BARROW. I know.
JIM. The taste of those pills! (ANN *sits* R. *of* KRAMER'S *desk.*)
BARROW. (*Leans over* JIM *again.*) Jim, how do you know there were 156 pills? (*No answer.*) Jim! Jim! (*Turns off lamp.*) That's a strange detail to remember—the number of those pills. It's so exact.
ANN. I don't understand it myself, doctor.
BARROW. (*Crosses back of* KRAMER'S *desk to* L. *of desk.*) Are you in the theater, too, Mrs. Downs?
ANN. I was. I was doing very well in the theater when I met Jim. When we married I felt one career in the family was enough—so I gave it up.
BARROW. (*Sits* L. *of* KRAMER'S *desk.*) Did Jim realize what that meant for you?
ANN. I think so.
BARROW. Do you regret it?
ANN. (*A brief pause—a bitter smile.*) We all have our vanity, doctor.
BARROW. Of course. Do you have any children?
ANN. No.
BARROW. How long have you been married?
ANN. Nine years. (*Suddenly bursts into tears.*) I love him, Dr. Barrow. I know he loves me.

BARROW. (*Leans over desk, puts hand on* ANN'S *hand to comfort her.*) That's good—that will help.

LIGHTS FADE QUICKLY

## ACT I

### Scene 3

*The same.*

TIME: *About noon, three days later: Friday.*

*A bright sun makes ward look almost cheerful. Saline bottle and stand should be removed, if possible—if not, needle disconnected from* JIM'S *arm, and whole stand moved slightly to rear of* JIM'S *bed.* GROSBERG *enters from* U. L. (*from between 2nd and 3rd legs on the left side*) *pushing a serving wagon on which are three trays, each containing a bowl of mush, technically known as a "soft diet," a cup of coffee, and a spoon.*

JIM *is sitting up in bed. From his attitude there is no awareness that anything at all unusual has taken place. Now that he's alive, the only thing that matters is to get out of the hospital as soon as possible. There is a strange combination of adult intelligence, good humor, and, at times, almost childish naïveté.*

GROSBERG *stops in front of* FLEMING'S *bed.*

FLEMING. What's for lunch? S.O.S.?
GROSBERG. (*In agreement, as he hands tray to* FLEMING.) S.O.S.
JIM. (*Tentatively.*) Mr. Grosberg?
GROSBERG. (*Back to wagon, pushes it in front of bed No. 1.*) What?
JIM. (*Through* GROSBERG'S *business.*) May I speak to you for a moment?
GROSBERG. (*Takes another tray from wagon.*) What do you want?
JIM. Would you do something for me?
GROSBERG. (*Puts tray on* JIM'S *lap.*) What?
JIM. (*Takes note from under his pillow, looks at* GROSBERG.) Would you see that this gets mailed?

GROSBERG. Your wife'll be here, won't she?—Why don't you ask her?
JIM. Well—I—I'd rather you did it. I —— Would you mind?
GROSBERG. (*Looks at* JIM.) That's worth a pack of cigarettes, at least.
JIM. I haven't got anything just now—but—I'd appreciate it.
GROSBERG. (*His hand out.*) Gi' me. (*Takes letter from* JIM, *starts back to wagon.*)
JIM. Thanks a million. (*Bell at door rings once.*)
GROSBERG. (*Puts letter in pocket as he goes L. to door, taking key from pocket.*) Where'd you get the paper and pencil?
JIM. (*An embarrassed smile—looks at* FLEMING.) I borrowed it.
GROSBERG. From Mr. Fleming?
FLEMING. (*To* GROSBERG.) There's no law against it, is there?
GROSBERG. (*As he opens door.*) Did I say anything? (*He admits* ANN, *who goes to L. of* JIM'S *bed.* GROSBERG *locks door after* ANN, *then goes back to wagon. He takes remaining tray, sits on L. side of bed No. 1, and begins to feed "patient" slowly.*)
FLEMING. (*As* ANN *crosses in front of* KRAMER'S *desk.*) Hi, Mrs. Downs?
ANN. (*Smiling.*) How are you, Mr. Fleming? (*Continues to* JIM.)
FLEMING. First-rate, Mrs. Downs.
ANN. (*At* JIM'S *bed.*) How do you feel, Jim?
JIM. Fine.
GROSBERG. You going to feed your husband again, Mrs. Downs?
JIM. I don't need anybody to feed me.
GROSBERG. (*Feeding the silent one—turns to* JIM.) You're a big boy now, huh? You weren't so big the last couple of days. Your wife did everything for you. (ANN *takes off her coat, puts it on chair L. of* JIM'S *bed, sits in this chair.*)
JIM. (*Looking at* ANN.) She did? (ANN *smiles at* JIM.) Thanks, Ann.
ANN. Eat your dinner. And then I have some wonderful news for you.
JIM. What?
ANN. Eat your dinner first.
JIM. Oh, Ann—that's not fair. What's the news?
ANN. The Joe Williams office called you.
JIM. What—for a job?
ANN. That's what they said. They want to see you.
JIM. When?
ANN. Monday afternoon. Naturally, I didn't tell them what happened.
JIM. Of course. Monday. That's wonderful! (*Moves tray away from him, and turns to* ANN, *as though wanting to get out of bed.*) Ann, I ought to try to get up—I ought to try to *walk.*

ANN. (*Laughs gently.*) Really, Jim—yesterday at this time you weren't able to sit up.
JIM. Will you let me try?
ANN. Please, Jim, don't. You're not strong enough.
JIM. (*Trying to get up.*) I know I can get up, Ann.
ANN. Eat your dinner first.
JIM. (*Hands tray to* ANN.) Let me stand for a minute, and then I'll eat.
ANN. (*Pushes tray back to* JIM, *gently.*) Jim—if the doctors thought you could get up, they'd let you.
JIM. Then let me talk to one of them. Is there a Dr. Barrow? I seem to remember that name. And a Dr. Kramer—is that right?
ANN. Yes. Dr. Kramer is your physician. He pulled you through.
JIM. If I could only talk to one of them. I feel much better now, Ann. Don't I *look* better to you? (BARROW *enters from down* R., *on way to* KRAMER'S *desk.*)
ANN. Much better.
JIM. Well?
ANN. (*Seeing* BARROW.) Oh, Dr. Barrow! Jim was just wanting to speak to you. (BARROW *stops, goes to* JIM, *to his* R.)
JIM. (*As* BARROW *comes to his bed.*) Are you Dr. Barrow? You're very attractive.
BARROW. (*Smiles, looks at* ANN.) What do you want?
JIM. I want to get up. I want to start walking around. I have an appointment on Monday—I'd like to keep it.
BARROW. Is it important?
JIM. It's for a job. That doesn't happen every day.
BARROW. Isn't it more important that you get well?
JIM. (*His look is pleading.*) It's the closest I've been to a job in God knows how long.
BARROW. With whom do you have this appointment?
JIM. With Mr. Williams—he's a producer.
BARROW. We can tell him you're ill.
JIM. Please don't tell him that. I'll be fine by Monday.
BARROW. Well, I can't say. I'm not your medical doctor. . . . I'm the psychiatrist. Dr. Kramer will have to pass on you physically.
JIM. May I see Dr. Kramer?
BARROW. He doesn't have the final say, either. Dr. Schlesinger—the chief psychiatrist on this floor—is the boss.
JIM. (*Hopefully.*) When will I see him?

BARROW. When Dr. Kramer says you're well. But I'll use whatever influence I can. When is the appointment?
JIM. On Monday.
BARROW. I'll try. I'll call Dr. Schlesinger now. (*Starts out* R.)
JIM. (*As* BARROW *goes.*) Thank you, Doctor. (BARROW *exits* D. R.)
ANN. Now—eat your dinner, Jim.
JIM. I'll drink my coffee. What do they call this stuff, anyway?
ANN. It's like baby food. They call it a soft diet. If you want to get up, you'd better eat—you'll need the strength.
JIM. Just one spoonful, that's all. (*Tastes food, grimaces.*)
ANN. (*Laughs.*) It's wonderful to see you in such good spirits again. When you come home, I'll make everything you like.
JIM. (*Stops, suddenly fearful.*) Ann—I'm not going to come home.
ANN. (*Silent for a moment—turns away from* JIM.) You can't go back to that cold-water flat—it's too depressing.
JIM. (*Urgently, but hushed.*) Ann, you're making a mistake. . . .
ANN. (*Rises, crosses below bed, to* R. *of* JIM'S *bed, casually brushing blanket at foot of bed as she goes.*) We don't have to discuss it now, Jim.
JIM. (*Louder, more agitated.*) I don't want to hurt you again—but you're taking it for granted I'll go back with you ——
ANN. (R. *of bed.*) It's all right, Jim. (KRAMER *lets himself in with his key. Locks door from inside.*)
JIM. (*Not aware of* KRAMER—*urgently, to* ANN.) It's *not* all right, Ann. I'm not ungrateful—but things are different ——
ANN. (*As she sees* KRAMER, *silences* JIM *with her hand.*) Here's Dr. Kramer.
KRAMER. (*Crossing* R., *on way to* JIM'S *bed.*) Good morning, Mrs. Downs. (*Comes to bed, to* L. *of* JIM.) How do you feel?
JIM. Fine. My wife has been telling me wonderful things about you, Dr. Kramer. I guess I owe my life to you.
KRAMER. I'm glad to hear you're grateful. You weren't for a while.
JIM. Doctor, I have a very important appointment on Monday. Do you think I'll be able to keep it?
KRAMER. (*Sits chair* L. *of* JIM'S *bed.*) When did *this* happen?
JIM. Just now. Ann took the call. I feel much better. Don't you think I can make it?
KRAMER. (*Thinking about it.*) Today's Friday—from the medical point of view it's quite likely you can leave by Monday. You've come along pretty well with your wife's help. You ought to be very grateful.

JIM. Yes, I know.
KRAMER. When I saw how well she was taking care of you I dismissed the special nurses.
JIM. Really? That's wonderful, Ann. Will you let me get up, Doctor? I'll show you I can do it. (DR. SCHLESINGER *and* DR. BARROW *enter from down* R. DR. SCHLESINGER *first, walks directly to* KRAMER'S *desk, picks up* JIM'S *chart which is in a manila folder on top of desk. He opens it, and while looking at it, walks a few steps to* L. *of chair at* L. *side of* KRAMER'S *desk.* BARROW *stops a few paces* L. *of* D. R. *entrance.*)
BARROW. (*Stops a moment.*) Mrs. Downs? (ANN *turns.*) May I see you a moment?
ANN. Of course. (ANN *crosses down to front of* KRAMER'S *desk to meet* SCHLESINGER.)
BARROW. Dr. Kramer? (*He turns to her.*) Please. (BARROW *now crosses* L. *to behind* KRAMER'S *desk.* KRAMER *pats* JIM *gently on shoulder, smiles at him, crosses to chair* R. *of his desk, and sits.*)
FLEMING. (*To* JIM.) The star chamber is in session. (*Through ensuing dialogue,* GROSBERG *goes to* FLEMING, *takes his tray, then to* JIM *and takes his tray. He puts trays on serving wagon. Then he gets tray from the "silent one," puts it on wagon, and pushes wagon off* R. JIM *and* FLEMING *lie down, ostensibly to nap after lunch.*)
SCHLESINGER. (*Having picked up chart from desk, turns to* ANN.) Mrs. Downs?
ANN. Yes.
SCHLESINGER. I'm Dr. Schlesinger.
ANN. How do you do?
SCHLESINGER. Won't you sit? (*To* ANN, *who sits chair* L. *of* KRAMER'S *desk.*) Have you any way of knowing whether this is a legitimate appointment or not?
ANN. Oh, yes. He has the appointment. The call came to me.
SCHLESINGER. I see. What do you think, Dr. Kramer?
KRAMER. Medically, I think it's possible.
SCHLESINGER. Dr. Barrow?
BARROW. Well, he said several times, in the unconscious state, he was a failure. Maybe if he got this job, it would be a healthy thing for him psychologically?
SCHLESINGER. (*Thumbing chart.*) Hm—hmm—perhaps it can be managed. (*Almost as an afterthought.*) Mrs. Downs, what do you think?
ANN. Of course, I'd like to see Jim get the job, but do you think it's possible?

SCHLESINGER. Why not?
ANN. Well, you would know these things better than I ——
SCHLESINGER. What's troubling you, Mrs. Downs?
ANN. Well, his eyes . . . they don't always seem to focus . . . (*Doctors look at each other.*)
BARROW. He sounds rational most of the time, doesn't he?
ANN. Yes—it's only once in a while he'll say something wild and incoherent.
SCHLESINGER. Like what?
ANN. I don't remember at the moment —— Doctor, what would happen if he kept the appointment and didn't get the job?
SCHLESINGER. Of course, it would be another failure, and that would be worse. (*Looks again at chart.*)
BARROW. Yes, that's true. But, somehow, if it's important ——
SCHLESINGER. And I see the chart indicates he said many times he would do it again.
KRAMER. Isn't that a normal reaction? I mean, it isn't at all unusual for a man to say such a thing unconsciously, so soon after making the attempt?
SCHLESINGER. Yes, I know, but ——
KRAMER. (*To* BARROW.) He hasn't said it since the first day, has he?
BARROW. (*Looks at* ANN.) No.
ANN. (*Reluctantly.*) No.
SCHLESINGER. It would still be a *great* risk.
KRAMER. We have until Monday.
BARROW. Suppose we see what happens. Dr. Kramer—you see what *you* can do about Mr. Downs, and we'll take it from there.
SCHLESINGER. (*Looks briefly at* KRAMER, *closes folder.*) I'll have a talk with him on Monday. (*To* ANN—KRAMER *rises impatiently, crosses upstage a few steps.*) I'd like to speak to you first, if possible, Mrs. Downs. Can you be in my office at eleven on Monday?
ANN. Certainly.
SCHLESINGER. Good. (*He and* BARROW *start* R. BARROW *crosses to nearly* C. *stage.* SCHLESINGER *crosses to just* R. *of* KRAMER'S *desk, stops, turns back to* ANN. BARROW *stops when he does.*) Oh, one more thing, Mrs. Downs. (*A step back.* BARROW *returns with him.*) I've been getting several phone calls a day from a Charlotte—somebody or other. She wants permission to see your husband. (*Pause.*)
BARROW. (*A step to* ANN.) If this girl is an emotional complication for your husband ——?

ANN. I—I don't know what to say. The whole thing is so humiliating to me.
SCHLESINGER. I must tell you, Mrs. Downs—as his wife—the law is entirely on your side. (*Another pause,* ANN *finally looks to* BARROW.)
ANN. I think it would be very bad for Jim to see her—don't you, Doctor?
BARROW. (*To* SCHLESINGER.) It *would* be a great strain.
SCHLESINGER. I quite agree. I'll leave word downstairs she's not to be admitted at any time. (SCHLESINGER *and* BARROW *turn* R., *go off* R. *together, in quiet ad lib consultation.* KRAMER *watches them go, then turns to* ANN.)
KRAMER. Come with me. (*They go back to* JIM'S *bed up* C., KRAMER *to* L., ANN *to* R. *With simulated enthusiasm.*) O.K., Jim. Let's see you go.
JIM. (*Sits up.*) What?
KRAMER. Come on, get dressed. Get out of bed. You're as healthy as I am.
ANN. (*Startled.*) Are you serious, Dr. Kramer?
KRAMER. (*With a wink to* ANN.) Of course I'm serious. Get him up.
JIM. Thank you, Doctor. (*He moves slowly to put his feet on floor.*)
ANN. (*All solicitude—gets slippers from under bed.*) Wait till I get these slippers on, dear.
FLEMING. (*Sits up in bed, shouts.*) Oh, no! What are they trying to do to the guy? Kill him?
KRAMER. Never mind, Mr. Fleming. Are you all right, Mr. Downs?
JIM. (*Has gotten out of bed—now standing* R. *side of bed.*) Fine—fine.
ANN. Hold on to me.
JIM. (*Holding* ANN'S *arm.*) You see, I'm up. (*Takes two or three steps.*)
FLEMING. Christ Almighty, he shouldn't be allowed—they're crazy!
JIM. (*When he reaches a step in front of his bed, he exults, like a small boy.*) I'm walking! I'm walking! (*His legs give away. Starts to slump. This is just exhaustion, a softening of the body, not sudden collapse.*)
ANN. (*Frightened—calls.*) Dr. Kramer! (KRAMER *quickly goes to* ANN'S *assistance, helps her place* JIM *on his bed.*)
KRAMER. (*Examines him, looks at his eyes, feels his pulse.*) He's asleep. He'll be all right. He'll be fine by Monday. (*Turns to* FLEMING, *smiles.*) Worried, Mr. Fleming? (*He crosses down* R., *exits* D. R.)
FLEMING. Those crazy bastards! I've never seen a hospital like this.

LIGHTS FADE QUICKLY

# ACT I

## Scene 4

SCENE: *Lights come up on* DR. SCHLESINGER'S *office—actually, just a table and two chairs in front of a hospital screen. The screen is the same one used to conceal* JIM'S *bed, only now the three folds are extended in a straight line and placed directly in* C. *stage, in front of the beds. The desk is* KRAMER'S *desk, which is moved quickly between scenes to in front of screen, in* C. *stage. Chairs at* KRAMER'S *desk are likewise moved at same time and placed again at* L. *and* R. *of desk.*

TIME: *11:00 A.M. Three days later, Monday.*

SCHLESINGER *is standing above desk,* C. ANN *is seated on* L.

SCHLESINGER. (*Crosses to* D. R. *of desk.*) Has he ever had periods of depression before?
ANN. Certainly not to this extent.
SCHLESINGER. (*Turns to* ANN.) Has he had psychiatric treatment before?
ANN. No. But I do think he needs help now.
SCHLESINGER. (*A step to* ANN.) Now tell me—has he spoken of doing this again?
ANN. Well—not in so many words, Doctor.
SCHLESINGER. I see. Do you think we should keep him in the hospital for a while?
ANN. It would help Jim immensely, I think, to get over this slowly. This is terribly important to me, Doctor. I feel he needs time—if he could be in the hospital's care for a while—I'm sure he'll realize our separation was a mistake.
SCHLESINGER. That may very well be. (*Crosses in front of desk to just* L. *of* ANN.) The other day you were reluctant to speak about Charlotte, Mrs. Downs.
ANN. Well—I can't help but feel that in some way she was responsible for this action.
SCHLESINGER. (*Turns to* ANN.) Mrs. Downs, your husband will be here in a minute. I'd rather he didn't see you. I want him to speak freely.
ANN. Of course. (ANN *rises, takes a step to* R.)
SCHLESINGER. (*Two or three steps to* ANN.) Your having been with him so much is of enormous help to us. I want to thank you, Mrs. Downs.

ANN. (*Smiles.*) Not at all. (*Turns, starts to exit* D. R.)
SCHLESINGER. I'd suggest you leave *this* way. (ANN *stops, turns*—
SCHLESINGER *indicates off* L.) You'll avoid running into him.
ANN. Thank you. (*She crosses in front of desk to* L., *starts to exit between 2nd and 3rd legs on* L.)
SCHLESINGER. You can wait in the next room. (ANN *turns, acknowledges* SCHLESINGER'S *direction, exits* U. L. SCHLESINGER *sits* R. *of desk—opens chart.* JIM *enters from* R.)
JIM. Dr. Schlesinger?
SCHLESINGER. Come in, Mr. Downs. (*Turns briefly to* JIM, *then back to chart. Pause.*) Sit down.
JIM. Thank you. (*Crosses front of desk, sits* L. *of desk.*)
SCHLESINGER. How do you feel?
JIM. Fine.
SCHLESINGER. (*Leans back.*) Well—I suppose you know you did a very serious thing? (JIM *shrugs, smiles.*) You don't think it was serious?
JIM. I—I've always known that suicide was considered a crime against the state. I never understood why.
SCHLESINGER. Is that all?
JIM. What else can I say? I did it—it didn't work—I'm alive now—that's all. I want to go home.
SCHLESINGER. (*Without looking at* JIM.) Why did you do this thing, Mr. Downs?
JIM. (*Didn't expect that kind of question.*) Well, it's a complicated business. It wasn't just *one* thing, it was a lot of things. This was the week-end before Thanksgiving. I was having a friend to dinner—it was Saturday night—I had spent practically my last cent—I was doing the cooking. When my friend arrived, she asked me what was for dessert. I didn't have any dessert. I couldn't afford it—and I started to cry.
SCHLESINGER. Do you cry easily? I mean, at other times?
JIM. No—not often.
SCHLESINGER. Well, not having dessert is hardly a reason to take your life.
JIM. I didn't mean to give that impression. It was simply an indication of how I stood. I had sixty cents left to last me eight days.
SCHLESINGER. (*Always looking for holes in the story.*) I understood you weren't working?
JIM. Not at my profession. I was teaching English privately and there was a check due in another week.
SCHLESINGER. All right—any other reasons?

JIM. A couple of years had passed since I did my last show—it didn't look as though I was ever going to get another one.
SCHLESINGER. I understand you have an appointment for a job—this afternoon, as a matter of fact.
JIM. Yes. It could be an important break.
SCHLESINGER. Hm—hmm—anything else?
JIM. I tried writing. Many years ago, while I was still in college, I was a newspaperman. And since I had the time, in the past few years, I mean—I thought I'd write. But nothing sold. I was working on a play, and I had finished the first act about a week before this happened. That Sunday night I re-read what I'd written. I don't know what made me do it—but I did. And I thought the whole thing was terrible. Everything just seemed hopeless.
SCHLESINGER. Why do you feel you're an old man?
JIM. (*Startled.*) When did I say that?
SCHLESINGER. In the unconscious state.
JIM. Really? (*Pause.*) Well—I guess I began to think about it when I was in the army. I was too old to become an officer. I forced myself to try and keep up with the younger men—it wasn't easy. I was made painfully aware of the difference.
SCHLESINGER. Were you overseas?
JIM. Yes—the whole European war—straight into Germany.
SCHLESINGER. I see. And when you came out of the army?
JIM. I found young men in the profession I didn't know. They didn't know me.
SCHLESINGER. But age is no deterrent in your work, Mr. Downs. There are very old people still active in the theater.
JIM. (*Irritated.*) Really, Doctor—I know that. But they aren't just starting out. I felt I was beginning all over again, and I thought I was too old for that.
SCHLESINGER. I see. Are those all the reasons?
JIM. I'm sorry, Doctor—I know people have gone on against greater difficulties. Everyone reaches a low at some time in their lives. I just gave in to it, that's all.
SCHLESINGER. But you said there were a lot of things. What about your wife?
JIM. Oh, yes—I remember. Sunday afternoon Ann called me. She said she wanted to talk to me, and we made a date for four o'clock the next afternoon—Monday.
SCHLESINGER. And when did you take the pills?

JIM. Monday morning, at about 11:30.
SCHLESINGER. Didn't you want to see your wife? (JIM shrugs.) Was your relationship so bad you couldn't even talk to her?
JIM. (Quickly.) No. I saw my wife several times after we separated. It was just—well, on top of everything I knew she needed money. I thought of my G.I. Insurance policy for ten thousand dollars. And I guess that clinched it. This was about twelve-thirty, that Sunday night. I wrote the first letter to my brother that night.
SCHLESINGER. There was more than one letter?
JIM. I only mailed one. When I had finished writing the letter, it occurred to me that I hadn't paid the November premium on my policy, so I figured I'd have to wait until the next morning.
SCHLESINGER. What for?
JIM. To check with the Veterans' Administration to see if my policy was still in force.
SCHLESINGER. Then what happened that night?
JIM. (Naively.) Nothing. I went to sleep.
SCHLESINGER. Didn't you have any thoughts of death? Weren't you disturbed in any way?
JIM. (Thinking about it.) No. I slept like a baby. In the morning I got up, went out for the morning papers—had coffee. I remember reading about a director who had been signed for a new show, and thinking he didn't have any talent at all.
SCHLESINGER. Yes. What happened next?
JIM. I phoned the Veterans' Administration and found out the policy was in force for thirty-one days after the last payment. So it was all right. I tore up the letter I wrote last night, and I wrote another one, giving my brother the information on the insurance.
SCHLESINGER. Did you give any reasons for taking your life?
JIM. No. Does a man ever really give reasons? (Pause. SCHLESINGER says nothing.) I enclosed the key to my apartment in the letter, addressed the envelope, and sealed it. Then—the only hesitation I had, was in when I should mail the letter—before, or after taking the pills. You see, I didn't know what effect the pills would have, or how fast they would work. So I thought—if I mailed the letter first and then lost courage, or the will to do it, all I would succeed in accomplishing would be to scare the hell out of a lot of people. So I decided to leave the letter on the kitchen table and leave the door to the apartment unlocked. If anyone came in and found me, they would see the letter. Then I went back to the living room, sat down on the edge of the bed,

and picked up the envelope with the pills. I looked at the pills for a minute, put them down again, and went to the kitchen for a glass of water. Then I went back to the bed, took a swallow of water—and then took all the pills.

SCHLESINGER. All at once?

JIM. I tried to. I emptied the pills from the envelope to my hand and took them all at one time. Several dropped on the floor and I even picked those up and took them, just to make sure.

SCHLESINGER. (*As if this question had never been asked before.*) How many pills did you take?

JIM. (*Simply.*) A hundred and fifty-six.

SCHLESINGER. (*His look says* JIM *is obviously lying.*) That's a strange number. How did you arrive at it?

JIM. (*His face is open—his tone honest.*) I didn't arrive at it, Doctor. That was the exact number.

SCHLESINGER. How do you know?

JIM. I counted them. Sunday night, I put them on the kitchen table in groups of ten, and I counted them.

SCHLESINGER. Why did you count them?

JIM. I had read in the papers several days before that some man had taken thirty-three pills and a lot of aspirin and all it did was to make him sick. I wanted to be sure I had enough.

SCHLESINGER. I see. Where did you get the pills?

JIM. I bought them.

SCHLESINGER. Where?

JIM. Different places—on Eighth Avenue.

SCHLESINGER. Did you have prescriptions?

JIM. No. I had no trouble at all—I just asked for them.

SCHLESINGER. Hm-hmmm. Now—to get back to that morning.

JIM. A week ago today, as a matter of fact. (*Smiles.*) Strange, isn't it?

SCHLESINGER. Yes—well—what happened after you took the pills?

JIM. Nothing. I was amazed. I didn't know what *should* happen, but nothing did.

SCHLESINGER. What thoughts did you have at *that* time?

JIM. None. None at all.

SCHLESINGER. You didn't think of anything? And yet, as far as you knew, you were dying?

JIM. I wondered whether I would have time now to mail the letter to my brother.

SCHLESINGER. *Then* what did you do?

JIM. I mailed it—and I got quite a kick out of doing it. It appealed to my sense of the dramatic, I guess. I walked down the street to the mail box on the corner, deposited the letter, and walked back to the apartment. And all the time I looked at the people on the street—I said good morning to people I knew—and I thought—they don't know it, but I'm a dying man. When I got back to the house, I locked the door of my apartment—I went into the living room, lay down on the bed, folded my arms under my head and crossed my legs—and then waited.

SCHLESINGER. What did you think about then?

JIM. Nothing. I was comfortable. It seemed the most comfortable bed I'd ever known.

SCHLESINGER. That's all?

JIM. I must have passed out about five or ten minutes later. It wasn't longer—I'm pretty sure of that. My wife and the police found me the next day—from what they tell me, it was just about twenty-four hours after I had taken the pills.

SCHLESINGER. (*Leans back again.*) Mr. Downs—what would you do if you got out of the hospital?

JIM. (*Frightened.*) I'd go home.

SCHLESINGER. Back to your wife?

JIM. (*Unable to understand the line.*) We were separated——

SCHLESINGER. I know—but after all she has done for you? You don't know it, Mr. Downs, but you were kept on the critical list long after it was necessary just to permit her to be with you.

JIM. I know—she told me.

SCHLESINGER. She must love you very much.

JIM. (*This is a struggle.*) Doctor—this may make me out an awful heel. But you don't know my wife. She makes a terrific impression on everyone. Not only in the hospital. It's been that way for years. Everybody thinks she's wonderful. I'm not trying to discount what she did for me here—but twenty-four hour a day living together over a period of years is a completely different story.

SCHLESINGER. If things are so difficult, why should she do—what she did for you?

JIM. This is going to sound even worse—but I can't help it. She wants to get me back, I suppose.

SCHLESINGER. But why? Don't you think she loves you?

JIM. (*Slowly.*) Maybe. But the fear of loneliness is a better reason. One time, in a quarrel—I forget what it was about—for bringing only one

salt and pepper shaker to the table instead of two, or dropping ashes on the floor—I forget now—I told her ——
SCHLESINGER. (*Interrupting.*) Just a minute.—You quarreled about such things?
JIM. Oh, yes—she wouldn't talk to me for days after such an argument, dropping something—anything.
SCHLESINGER. What did you tell her?
JIM. I told her she'd probably end up a lonely old woman. I think she's afraid of that. My wife is the same age as me—forty-two, and at that age the fear of loneliness can be a very real thing. She has a couple of friends—the only real friends she has, as a matter of fact—and they are alone. She knows what loneliness has done to these women—it's a terrible curse. I guess, even having someone to fight with is better than being lonely.
SCHLESINGER. (*Brief pause—pointedly.*) Then you don't think going back to your wife would mean a more stable life for you?
JIM. There was no stability before—why should there be now? (*In reflection.*) My wife's a very possessive woman—it took me a long time to get out of her clutches.
SCHLESINGER. (*Quietly.*) Who is Charlotte?
JIM. (*Stunned.*) Charlotte?
SCHLESINGER. Yes, Charlotte—who is she?
JIM. (*Still shocked.*) A—a friend.
SCHLESINGER. The friend who came to dinner that Saturday night?
JIM. Yes.
SCHLESINGER. (*Toying with his pen.*) You tried to have a letter mailed to her. Didn't you know that was against the rules?
JIM. How did you know about the letter? Did Grosberg . . . ?
SCHLESINGER. Yes, Mr. Grosberg gave me your letter. That's part of his job—keeping an eye on the patients. You must understand that when you are brought here for suicide you give up certain rights to privacy.
JIM. There was no harm in the letter—I just asked her to visit me, that's all. I can't understand why she hasn't been here.
SCHLESINGER. Oh, she's been here all right, and she's been pestering me with phone calls. We haven't thought it wise for you to see her.
JIM. Who's we? My wife?
SCHLESINGER. No, Dr. Barrow and myself. Are you involved with this **girl**?
JIM. How do you mean—involved?

SCHLESINGER. Are you in love with her?
JIM. I don't know what you're getting at.
SCHLESINGER. Do you *think* you're in love with her?
JIM. Well ——
SCHLESINGER. Aren't my questions clear?
JIM. Yes, they are—but it seems like an awful lot of prying. If—if I'm well—I'd like to go home.
SCHLESINGER. Why don't you want to answer my questions?
JIM. I'll cooperate in any way I can, Doctor—but I fail to see why Charlotte has to be brought into this.
SCHLESINGER. (*Making note.*) Hm-hmmmm.
JIM. (*While* SCHLESINGER *is writing.*) May I go home, Doctor? May I keep my appointment?
SCHLESINGER. I'm afraid it may have to be postponed, Mr. Downs.
JIM. Why? For God's sake. This is the most vital appointment of my life.
SCHLESINGER. I'm going to transfer you to another ward for a few days. (SCHLESINGER *rises.*) Now, if you don't mind, look at my finger, please. (*He holds his index finger upright, about twelve inches before* JIM'S *eyes and moves it from* L. *to* R. *several times.* JIM *moves his head in direction of the moving finger.*) Not the head, please—just the eyes. (*Starts again, moving finger slowly at first, to about twelve inches on either side of* JIM'S *nose, then more quickly and with shorter strokes. When he is satisfied [three or four moves all told]—he sits down again. Then, as he writes.*) It's a convalescent ward, on the first floor. You'll like it. You can wear your own clothes there, instead of these hospital things. They play games down there—all sorts of interesting things. It's only for a few days.
JIM. (*Dazed—still sitting.*) I see.
SCHLESINGER. That will be all, Mr. Downs. (*Slowly* JIM *rises, starts off* R. *When he has crossed in front of the desk to* R. *of* SCHLESINGER, *he stops, turns back to look at* SCHLESINGER, *who is still writing—then, bewildered and numb, he exits* D. R.)

## LIGHTS FADE QUICKLY

## ACT I

### Scene 5

SCENE: *The whole ward.*

TIME: *Immediately following.*

*The screen has been moved back to its original position, and* KRAMER'S *desk and two chairs are likewise restored to their positions.*

ON:

GROSBERG *sits on bed of the staring one, filing his nails.*

FLEMING *is in bed.*

MISS HANSEN *is sitting at her desk.*

JIM, *despondent, comes in from* R. *and goes to* L. *side of his bed.*

FLEMING. (*When* JIM *enters.*) What's the matter, Downs?
JIM. Nothing.
FLEMING. Nothing! Christ, you look like ——
JIM. (*Restless, disturbed, fools with blanket on his bed.*) I thought I was going home today.
FLEMING. What did he say?
JIM. I'm being transferred to the first floor—for a few days.
FLEMING. A few days, my foot. Everything around here's for a few days—the short way of saying indefinitely. You're going to "One." That's the observation ward. Nobody goes there for just a few days.
JIM. (*Quietly—not enjoying the gag.*) O.K. O.K.
FLEMING. You're in the psycho building, Downs. Didn't you know that?
JIM. (*Suddenly—as though struck—turns to* FLEMING.) *Psycho* building!
FLEMING. I guess you've been too sick to notice.
JIM. Notice what?
FLEMING. Look around you, for Christ's sake. Hey, Grosberg—tell this guy what MN1 is like.
GROSBERG. (*To* JIM.) Is that where you're going?
JIM. (*Turns to him.*) Why did you turn in my letter? Why didn't you tell me first?

GROSBERG. (*Rises.*) I'm sorry—that's my job. (*He puts file away, takes comb from his pocket, combs hair of staring one.*) You'll like it in "One," Mr. Downs. It's a convalescent ward. You can wear your own clothes—they play games down there and everything.
FLEMING. Grosberg, cut it out. Tell this guy where he's going.
GROSBERG. (*Softening the blow—turns to* JIM, *takes step to him.*) It's not bad, really, Mr. Downs. It's the nicest ward—lots of people go home from there.
JIM. (*Frightened.*) And if they don't go home?
GROSBERG. (*Quietly.*) State Hospital.
FLEMING. He didn't know he was in the psycho building.
GROSBERG. Oh, yes. Didn't you notice the windows, Mr. Downs? (*Points to one.*) This heavy screen in front? You see, you can't reach the window at all.
JIM. (*Dully.*) It never occurred to me.
GROSBERG. (*Steps to foot of bed, points to door.*) And the locked door? You didn't notice that?
JIM. (*Turns to door.*) Yes—I noticed it. I don't know why—it never occurred to me. (*To* GROSBERG.) Do all suicides come here?
GROSBERG. If they need medical care. (*Returns to patient, combing hair.*)
JIM. Can you go right home from this ward?
GROSBERG. Yes, Mr. Downs, that's happened.
JIM. Then it isn't hospital procedure that a suicide is automatically sent to observation?
GROSBERG. (*A brief pause—simply.*) No. (*Bell at door rings once.* MISS HANSEN *rises immediately to open it.*)
JIM. (*Runs up to* L. *side of his bed, to* GROSBERG. *Cries out.*) But why? What did I say? What did I do?
GROSBERG. I don't know, Mr. Downs.
JIM. I told the truth about everything.
GROSBERG. I'm not the psychiatrist.
JIM. Can they keep me here—just like that—for no reason? (*Door has been opened by* MISS HANSEN, *admitting* ANN, *who presents her pass.*)
MISS HANSEN. (*Looks briefly at pass, then calls out.*) Downs!
JIM. (*Turns—sees* ANN, *runs to her, terror-stricken. They meet in* C. *stage.*) Ann—they're putting me away! They think I'm insane.
ANN. It's only for a few days.
JIM. (*A step back.*) A few days?

ANN. What's the matter?
JIM. (*Horrified*.) You knew! (*Draws away from her—a chill runs through him as he looks at her.*) You knew about this!

## CURTAIN

## ACT II

### Scene 1

SCENE: *Ward MN1, City Hospital.*

*Essentially, it's the same ward we saw before. Structurally, it's exactly the same. But down here, the beds are made. All but one, which is bare but for the mattress.*

TIME: *The next day, Tuesday.*

*Some patients are wearing their own clothes—others are in hospital pajamas. No one wears a necktie, but more conspicuously, no one wears a belt. To hold his trousers up, regular or pajama trousers, each man is given a length of white gauze bandage.*

*There are seven beds in this ward, numbered from R. to L., No. 1, No. 2, No. 3, No. 4, No. 5, No. 6, across the stage, where beds in Act I were placed. A seventh bed is placed down R., parallel to footlights, head of the bed facing C., foot extending slightly off-stage. Entrances from R. are made between this bed and foot of bed No. 1. Beds are occupied as follows:* O'BRIEN, *No. 1;* SCHLOSS, *No. 2;* TAGER, *No. 3; JIM, No. 4;* ANKORITIS, *No. 5;* MAJOR, *No. 6;* CARLISLE, *No. 7.* MISS HANSEN'S *desk remains where it was.*

*When curtain rises,* MAJOR, *a powerfully built but wonderfully graceful Negro, in his early thirties, is sitting on his bed, facing C., singing quietly a plaintive folk tune.* ANKORITIS, *a swarthy Greek, is sitting back on his bed, reading newspaper.* O'BRIEN, *a small, thin, dark-complexioned boy of twenty, with a pronounced Spanish accent, is sitting on L. side of his bed, drawing from memory, with a pencil, on medium-sized drawing pad. Several of his drawings are lying on* SCHLOSS' *bed. In a moment* TAGER, *a Jewish boy, about thirty-five, enters from R., carrying towel. He is drying his hands as he goes to metal cabinet L. of his bed. Puts towel away, and as he turns* to R., *notices drawings on bed No. 2. He goes to* L. *of bed No. 2, picks up a drawing, looks at it briefly, then turns to* O'BRIEN. MAJOR *continues to sing softly.*

TAGER. Did you do this?
O'BRIEN. (*That Spanish accent is thick—he speaks rapidly.*) You like it? I never painted before in my life. You know who it is? The nurse with the smile—you know who I mean? The doctor say I should paint, I have ideas, I have talent—I like to paint.
TAGER. Where'd you get the name O'Brien?
O'BRIEN. My father, he was Irish. He left my mother before I was born.
TAGER. Where was this?
O'BRIEN. (*Stands up, bed No. 2 is between* TAGER *and* O'BRIEN.) Havana, Cuba.
TAGER. Your mother alive?
O'BRIEN. No—she die when I am born. My aunt tell me everything when I grow up.
TAGER. (*Has been looking at drawings.*) Hey! *This* is good.
O'BRIEN. When I get out I'm going to school—I get thousand dollar a picture when I learn. (*Takes drawing back to his bed.* TAGER *sits on his bed,* R., *and shuffles a pack of cards aimlessly. Door is opened from outside with a key, and* JIM *enters, dressed as he was upstairs, followed by* DON GREGORY, *a tall, slender, young man of twenty-four.* GREGORY *is dressed in army sun-tans, the improvised uniform of an attendant. He carries* JIM'S *charts.* JIM *enters slowly, a few steps beyond door.* O'BRIEN *and* TAGER *look at him casually.* ANKORITIS *lowers his newspaper.* MAJOR *stops singing.*)
GREGORY. (*As he locks door.*) We'll find you a bed first, then I'll take these charts to the office. We're pretty crowded—we've got beds in the halls. (*Crosses* JIM *to* L. C.) There's no bed in here, is there, fellows?
TAGER. Yeah—next to me.
GREGORY. (*Crosses to between beds No. 3 and No. 4. Bed No. 4 is unmade, with sheets and blanket crumpled in a heap in center of bed.*) Whose bed was it?
TAGER. O'Malley, the cop.
GREGORY. (U. R. *of bed—surprised.*) Did he go home? (JIM *crosses few steps to* L. C.)
TAGER. Yeah, about an hour ago.
GREGORY. I'm glad for him. (*Looks at bed.*) There's no pillow. (*Gathers up used linen and blanket—addresses* JIM.) I'll see if I can get you

one. You have to keep your eyes open and grab one as soon as somebody leaves. (*Crosses to* R. JIM *automatically follows him.* GREGORY *turns to him.*) No—you stay here for now, Mr. Downs. I'll get your linen. (*Takes step to* R., *stops.*) And pajamas. Nobody's dressed like that down here. (*Leaves* R. *Pause.*)
MAJOR. (*After a beat, looks at* JIM, *rises.*) Your name Downs?
JIM. (*His eyes uncertain, bewildered—quietly, turns to* MAJOR.) Yes.
MAJOR. Mine's Major. Glad to know you. (*Shakes hands with* JIM *across* ANKORITIS' *bed.*)
TAGER. (*Simply waves to him.*) Sam Tager.
O'BRIEN. (*Also waving.*) George O'Brien.
ANKORITIS. My name is John Ankoritis. I do not know how well versed you are in the sound of names, Mr. Downs—so I will tell you that I am Greek, and very proud of the heritage of my Hellenic ancestors.
JIM. (*Softly.*) You should be.
ANKORITIS. (*A broad smile.*) Thank you. (*To others.*) We have a scholar in our midst, gentlemen. (*To* JIM.) Would you like to see a copy of this morning's Times? It is at your disposal.
JIM. (*Standing* L. *of his bed, turns, crosses down to foot of bed.*) Thank you—I—I have a slight headache. Later, maybe.
ANKORITIS. May a thousand blessings descend upon your head, Mr. Major.
MAJOR. (*Sits* R. *side of his bed.*) What for?
ANKORITIS. I have been in this pesthole for ten days and no one has ever thought to start introductions before. I like it. We must maintain the custom.
MAJOR. (*Takes cigarettes from pocket of his pajamas.*) Just being friendly, that's all.
ANKORITIS. Excellent. Have you a cigarette? (*Takes cigarette from* MAJOR, *produces matches from his own pocket, lights* MAJOR'S, *then his own.*)
GREGORY. (*Through this business, enters* R. *with linen and pillow.*) I've got you a pillow. I'll help you make the bed. (*Throws open a sheet.*) The fellows make their own beds every morning. Were you in the army?
JIM. Yes.
GREGORY. (R. *of* JIM'S *bed, helps* JIM *with making bed.*) Then you know how it is. Shaves three times a week. Showers every visiting day. (GREGORY *sees the smoke—to* ANKORITIS *and* MAJOR.) Now you fel-

lows know you're not supposed to smoke in the ward. Go to the john or the day-room—and give me the matches.
ANKORITIS. (*Throws him matches.* GREGORY *puts them in his pocket.*) I have more.
GREGORY. Don't let me see them. You can always ask me for a light—you know that.
MAJOR. You're not always around. (CARLISLE *enters from* L., *above door* L. *He is an old man, past sixty—a Negro. The gentlest man in the world, with a soft, slow voice. He crosses slowly to* R., *to his bed.*)
GREGORY. Then ask one of the other attendants. You know I'm supposed to report this—why do you do it? If someone else catches you, you'll wind up on "Seven."
MAJOR. (*Laughing.*) You're always scaring us with Seven. (*An authoritative voice offstage calls* "*Mr. Gregory!*")
GREGORY. Watch out for your butts—will you, fellows? (*Crosses* R.,—*as he passes* CARLISLE.) How are things, Mr. Carlisle?
CARLISLE. Fine—fine. (GREGORY *exits* R.) Them student nurses—they want to play cards all the time. (*Lies down on his bed, facing* C.)
MAJOR. They're supposed to do that, Mr. Carlisle. That's their job.
CARLISLE. I know it's their job—but I don't want to play cards.
ANKORITIS. (*Moves to front of his bed.*) They want to engage you in conversation, my dear Mr. Carlisle.
CARLISLE. I *know* that.
ANKORITIS. They wish to extract information which they in turn pass on to the esteemed physicians.
CARLISLE. (*Gently.*) I know all that.
O'BRIEN. Everything you say and do down here gets reported.
TAGER. You ain't kidding. They don't miss a trick. Somebody's always watching you.
CARLISLE. I just want to be left alone. I don't like dominoes or Chinese Checkers, or any games.
ANKORITIS. Then convey your displeasure in the most tactful manner, Mr. Carlisle.
CARLISLE. I did that—I told them I don't like to play games.
TAGER. That's the trouble in this place. Nobody treats you like a human being. You're a patient—you're being observed.
MAJOR. (*Rising—to* TAGER.) In here we're special—everything we do has a meaning. (TAGER *shows deck of cards to* MAJOR, *implying* "*Do you want to play?*" MAJOR *crosses to* TAGER'S *bed.*)

O'BRIEN. (*Seriously—without a pause.*) That's right. Just because you act a little crazy is no reason to say that you *are*.
ANKORITIS. It is the penalty, my dear Mr. O'Brien, of official surveillance. We lacked the wisdom to avoid being incarcerated.
O'BRIEN. Nobody sent *me* here. I came here by myself. (CARLISLE *turns, looks at* O'BRIEN.)
ANKORITIS. You're mad, my dear boy.
O'BRIEN. (*On his bed.*) That's true. I knew I was run-down, and a friend of mine told me I could come here for a physical check-up. (*Rises, crosses to front of bed No. 2.*) He said ask any policeman and he will take you to the hospital. So I did, and he brought me to the hospital, and the nurse asked me what I wanted, and I told her a physical check-up, and they sent me here. That's the truth.
CARLISLE. Anybody walks in here by himself ought to go straight to Seven. (O'BRIEN *goes back to his bed.*)
TAGER. Don't *say* that, Mr. Carlisle. You don't know what it's like on Seven.
JIM. (*Making his bed, stops—looks at* TAGER—*finally gets courage to ask.*) What's Seven?
TAGER. (*Stops playing cards, looks at* JIM.) The seventh floor. It's the violent ward. (JIM *stands still, listens.*) I was in a straight-jacket up there. I tried to throw myself in front of a subway train. Some cops grabbed me and I put up a fight—which I know now was a stupid thing to do. The next thing I know, I'm up on Seven in a straight-jacket. (*Seriously.*) Did you see that movie, "The Snake Pit"? Well, they didn't exaggerate nothin'. My family saw it, and they said—Aw, it's only a movie. They should know. *Nobody* knows till you see it from the inside. There was a guy up there who used to dance on one foot and play the fiddle—an imaginary fiddle—like this —— (*Rises—imitates him—others watch soberly.*) And there was one guy who used to go around as if he was looking in windows and he'd wave at somebody through the window—like this —— (*Again the imitation—then turns to* JIM.) You put that in a movie and people laugh. What's funny about that, will you tell me? (*Brief pause. They are quite serious. He sits slowly on his bed,* R.) I don't wish it on my worst enemy, they should go to Seven. (*The men are affected.* JIM *forces himself to go on making his bed.*)
SCHLOSS. (*A medium-sized gentleman from the "Greenpernt" section of Brooklyn enters in a hurry,* R.) Where's the new guy?
TAGER. (*Pointing.*) Right here.

SCHLOSS. I finished anudder chapter on my novel. (*Goes to his cabinet up* R. *of* TAGER'S *bed.*)
ANKORITIS. Doesn't the poetic muse inspire you any more, Mr. Schloss?
SCHLOSS. (*Crosses to* R. *of* JIM'S *bed, with dime store copy-book in his hand.*) I'm finished wit' poetry. I'm writin' a novel. I got two chapters done since breakfast. (*To* JIM.) What's your name?
JIM. (*Stops making bed, crosses to foot of it.*) Downs.
SCHLOSS. Mr. Downs, I hear you're in the theayter.
JIM. Where did you hear that?
SCHLOSS. It gets around fast. If you're in the theayter, you must be interested in literature. I want you should hear this here chapter. (*Reads from copy-book.*) "So Captain Redbeard faced his bunch of cut-throats—the most villainous scoundrels that sailed the Seven Seas—and he says 'Avast, me hearties, we are about to attack the good ship Avalon, which it is loaded with gold and silver from the Spanish Main.'" How do you like it?
JIM. You just started.
SCHLOSS. I mean, so far?
JIM. It's good.
SCHLOSS. The ideas just come to me, whereupon I write 'em. This here chapter's full of action.
JIM. It's good—you should continue.
SCHLOSS. That's what the doctor tells me. He says I got ideas—I just gotta learn some grammar, that's all. Would you believe it, I never did no writin' before?
ANKORITIS. This place must agree with you, Mr.—eh—Mr.—eh ——?
SCHLOSS. Schloss is the name. (*Crosses* R., *to his own bed.*) No, this place stinks—it's worse than jail.
TAGER. (*Playing casino with* MAJOR.) Have you been to jail?
SCHLOSS. (*Standing* U. L. *of his bed.*) Sure. I give Uncle Sam two years in Leavenworth one time. And I give him eighteen months in Atlanta.
MAJOR. What do you mean, you *give* him?
SCHLOSS. (*Turns to him—angrily.*) He wanted it—so I gave it to him!
MAJOR. What for?
SCHLOSS. Defraudin' the govament. In jail, at least you know when you're gettin' out. In this God-damn place you never know nothin'. (*Turning pages of his tablet.*) Would you like to hear some of my poetry, Mr. Downs? "There is a nurse with smile so warm, but the smile conceals a heart so cold. She smiles so warm, it makes you bold,

but then you find out her heart is cold." That's only the first voise—there's more.

TAGER. What are you doing in this ward, Mr. Schloss? There's nothing wrong with you.

SCHLOSS. (*Sits on his bed, facing* C.) Aaaaah, I slugged the wife and kids, so the cops trun me in here.

O'BRIEN. You should be ashamed to admit it, Mr. Schloss.

SCHLOSS. (*Without looking at him.*) You shut your mouth, you Spic bastard!

O'BRIEN. (*Rises.*) Take that back!

SCHLOSS. (*Calmly, as he puts tablet on his bed, rises, crosses down to* L. *of his bed.*) Ya lousy little bastard! Where do you come off with a name like O'Brien? (*Turns to* O'BRIEN.) Your mother was a Spic whore—that's what she was.

O'BRIEN. (*Fighting his tears—takes step to* SCHLOSS.) She was not. My mother was a good woman, she was a good —— (*Sputters his rage.*) You—you —— (*He rushes to* SCHLOSS, *who grabs* O'BRIEN'S *shoulders, pushes him to floor.* ANKORITIS *crosses* R. *to* SCHLOSS, *pulls him off.* CARLISLE *helps* O'BRIEN *to his feet.* TAGER *and* MAJOR *rise when fight starts.* TAGER *tries to take* ANKORITIS *away from* SCHLOSS. MAJOR *crosses down to* C., *facing them.*)

SCHLOSS. (*As* ANKORITIS *pulls him away from* O'BRIEN.) You take your crummy hands off me.

TAGER. (*Holding* ANKORITIS *away.*) Let him go, Mr. Ankoritis!

MAJOR. (*Furious, but staying clear of fight.*) There ain't one of us here who wouldn't like to break Mr. Schloss' neck ——

SCHLOSS. Yeah? Try it.

MAJOR. (*A step to* SCHLOSS.) But we're the ones who'd wind up in Seven—not him.

TAGER. (*Rushes to* MAJOR *to keep him out of trouble.*) Shut up, Mr. Major.

ANKORITIS. (*Quietly—with venom.*) It makes me sick to my stomach to look at you, Mr. Schloss.

SCHLOSS. (*Turns away.*) Aaah! (*Goes* U. R. *to his bed.*)

GREGORY. (*Enters from* R. *with chart to place on* HANSEN'S *desk—senses the silence—slows his walk, crosses to* TAGER.) What happened?

TAGER. (*Covering for everyone.*) A few words.

GREGORY. (*Looks slowly around at everyone, then as he continues to* HANSEN'S *desk.*) Just keep it to words, boys—and no one will get hurt

Time for lunch, everybody. Let's go! (*Group breaks up, each going to his bed.*)

JIM. (*Anxiously as he crosses down to* R. *of* GREGORY.) Mr. Gregory. How soon can I see a doctor? (*All but* SCHLOSS *turn to* JIM *and* GREGORY, *and watch quietly.*)

GREGORY. I don't know. They're way behind in interviews now.

JIM. How long do you think? I want to get out of here.

GREGORY. A few days maybe.

JIM. Before I even *see* a doctor?

GREGORY. It may be a few days before you're even assigned to a doctor. (JIM *turns away in impatience.* GREGORY *takes step to him.*) You'd better learn to be patient, Mr. Downs, if you want to get out of here. You start being anxious and you'll beat your head against the wall.

JIM. (*Furious—turns back to* GREGORY.) Oh, my God, why? Why? Why was I sent here in the first place?

GREGORY. There isn't a patient in this building who doesn't feel like you do.

JIM. (*Almost shouts.*) But I'm not —— (*Stops suddenly in full realization—looks at* GREGORY—*then quietly.*) I see—no one else thinks he is, either.

GREGORY. That's right. In this place, *they* don't have to prove that you are—*you* have to prove that you're not. Chow, fellows. Are you all here? (*A glance around, then he pats* JIM'S *arm gently, exits* R. *Men ad lib their response—get up and start for exit* R., SCHLOSS *first, and quickly,* O'BRIEN *helps* CARLISLE *out of bed, and they leave.* MAJOR *joins* TAGER, *and they go. Finally,* ANKORITIS *comes to* L. *of* JIM, *pats his arm.*)

ANKORITIS. (*As he leaves.*) You see, Mr. Downs, we are all *here*, but the question is, are we all *there*? (JIM, *standing alone, slowly follows* R.)

## LIGHTS FADE QUICKLY

## ACT II

### Scene 2

SCENE: *Once more, lights pick out only a desk and two chairs—the cubbyhole of an office. The rest of the stage is dark. This is precisely the same set-up that was used for the* SCHLESINGER *scene. The screen,* KRAMER'S *desk, which is off-*

*stage in this act, but will be brought on for this scene, and two chairs.*

TIME: *The next day—Wednesday—after lunch.*

DR. BELLMAN *seated back of desk* C. *He is a young man, not more than thirty-two or three. Wears glasses.*

JIM *enters from* R., *wearing pajamas, top and bottom. He comes to* R. *of desk.*

BELLMAN. (*Who has been reading a medical journal until* JIM *enters, looks up.*) Are you Mr. Downs?
JIM. Yes, sir.
BELLMAN. (*Closing journal.*) Sit down, please.
JIM. Thank you.
BELLMAN. How do you feel?
JIM. Fine.
BELLMAN. Now tell me about this business.
JIM. The whole thing?
BELLMAN. Whatever you want to say. Why did you do it?
JIM. Isn't it down in the chart? I gave all the details to Dr. Schlesinger.
BELLMAN. I know—but I want you to tell *me*. What were the circumstances that morning?
JIM. (*Trying to be patient.*) The circumstances were that I was fed up with being out of work, I didn't think I was ever going to work again, my wife wanted money, and I figured the way to give it to her was to take my life.
BELLMAN. Your G.I. insurance?
JIM. Yes.
BELLMAN. How many pills did you take?
JIM. A hundred and fifty-six. Why is that such a puzzler, Doctor? Everybody makes so much of that.
BELLMAN. (*Ignores question.*) How do you know there were exactly a hundred and fifty-six?
JIM. (*Rebuffed.*) I counted them.
BELLMAN. Why?
JIM. Because I had read some guy had taken thirty-three pills and a load of aspirin, and it only made him sick. I wanted to be sure I had enough.

BELLMAN. Do you frequently get periods of deep depression?
JIM. No—no more than most people.
BELLMAN. I mean you, personally.
JIM. No.
BELLMAN. Do you ever have periods of great elation?
JIM. I'm not manic-depressive, Doctor—if that's what these questions are intended to elicit.
BELLMAN. (*Momentarily startled, but tries to conceal this from* JIM.) Well—what exactly were you thinking about when you went through the preparation for this act?
JIM. Nothing—just what was happening at the moment.
BELLMAN. Don't you think that's strange?
JIM. Not at all. It was a conscious decision. I made up my mind to do it, and that was that.
BELLMAN. Didn't you think of how other people would feel when they found out?
JIM. No—I'm not really that important to any one.
BELLMAN. Didn't you think your wife would be hurt?
JIM. Not really. She'd have gotten over it very quickly.
BELLMAN. And—Charlotte?
JIM. Well—yes—but it wouldn't last. No such hurt lasts, except as an affectation.
BELLMAN. Why do you say that?
JIM. It's true. (*Brief pause.*) The world would soon come to a stop if all the dead were continually mourned.
BELLMAN. (*Looks at* JIM *a moment.*) I see. (*Brief pause.*) Do you know you have a reputation for being belligerent and nasty?
JIM. (*Puzzled.*) I have?
BELLMAN. Yes.
JIM. I'm sorry, Doctor. I had always thought of myself as an easy person to get along with. I think my friends would say that about me.
BELLMAN. Maybe they don't know you well enough.
JIM. May I ask—who told you I had such a reputation?
BELLMAN. People who know you well.
JIM. But who can they be?
BELLMAN. Your wife knows you well, doesn't she?
JIM. (*Slowly.*) Yes. I suppose.
BELLMAN. Is it true?
JIM. Well, that's hardly for me to say, is it? I'm sorry she feels that way.

BELLMAN. Your wife says, also, you are frequently wild and incoherent.
JIM. (*Disturbed.*) I'm wild and incoherent? Honest to God!
BELLMAN. What's the matter, Mr. Downs?
JIM. Either you're making this up to see how I'll behave, or something has happened to my wife. We were separated, I know, but I can't believe she'd *say* such things about me.
BELLMAN. Then you don't think it's true?
JIM. Of course it's not true.
BELLMAN. Tell me about Charlotte, will you?
JIM. She's a girl I fell in love with. Now, is that so unusual?
BELLMAN. What sort of girl is she?
JIM. (*Beginning to lose control.*) Look, Dr. Bellman. I'll answer any question you like about the attempt on my life—I *have* answered—as completely as I can—*all* your questions. But Charlotte has nothing to do with this.
BELLMAN. You must allow me to decide that, Mr. Downs.
JIM. *I want to go home.* I'm perfectly well now.
BELLMAN. (*Quietly.*) In time, Mr. Downs. You must have patience. (*A breath.*) Everyone in the hospital speaks very well of your wife—she was extremely devoted in your first critical days here.
JIM. I know. Everybody tells me Ann is a fine person.
BELLMAN. Did you ever try to give up Charlotte?
JIM. A dozen times. I didn't *want* to hurt Ann—I tried to go on living with her. That only made it worse. I was miserable with Charlotte and I was miserable at home.
BELLMAN. So you finally took your own apartment?
JIM. Yes.
BELLMAN. How long were you living alone before this happened?
JIM. About three months.
BELLMAN. (*Making notes.*) I see.
JIM. I've answered your questions, Doctor. May I go home?
BELLMAN. (*Still writing.*) Just a minute.
JIM. I don't belong here—you can see that.
BELLMAN. Of course. Just a few more questions. Who's the Mayor of New York?
JIM. (*At once.*) Impelliteri.
BELLMAN. Who's the President of the United States?
JIM. Truman.
BELLMAN. Who was the President before him?
JIM. Roosevelt.

BELLMAN. When did President Roosevelt die?
JIM. (*Looks at* BELLMAN, *incredulously.*) Doctor—you don't really think I'm insane, do you?
BELLMAN. Just answer my questions—when did Roosevelt die?
JIM. April—April —— (*A pause.*) April—12th—1945.
BELLMAN. What is the capital of France?
JIM. Paris.
BELLMAN. What does the expression—A rolling stone gathers no moss—mean to you?
JIM. Well—it means that—a person who wanders around a great deal doesn't plant any roots—has no foundation—doesn't gather any of the moss of well-being, if you want to put it that way—of stability.
BELLMAN. I see. And the expression—People who live in glass houses shouldn't throw stones?
JIM. That means—people of equal guilt, for the same fault, perhaps—shouldn't hurl accusations at each other.
BELLMAN. Hm-hmm. Now subtract by sevens from a hundred.
JIM. You've finally hit a weak spot.
BELLMAN. Go ahead.
JIM. (*This is slow and painful.*) Ninety-three—eighty-four—seventy-seven—seventy—sixty-three—fifty—fifty-six—forty-nine—forty-two—thirty-five—twenty-eight—twenty-one—fourteen—seven—zero. (JIM *is agitated.*) I want to tell you a story, Doctor.
BELLMAN. What is it?
JIM. (*He knows he is saying wrong thing, but seems driven by some relentless force.*) Four years ago I knew a doctor—a young psychiatrist in exactly your position—attached at that time to another City Hospital. He wanted me to write a play with him based on some of his case histories. One day, while he was making the rounds, he stopped in this screened-in porch, and he asked one of the patients—what day is today? The girl didn't answer, and he said—Do you know who I am? She still didn't answer, but I could see the disgust in her face. Then one of the *other* patients answered—an older woman. She turned around and said —— (*Imitating the sarcasm in a high voice.*) Who's the Mayor of New York? Who's the Governor of the State? Who's the President of the United States?
BELLMAN. (*Confused for a moment.*) Well—what does that prove?
JIM. To me, Doctor—particularly since—ironically—I find myself four years later in exactly the same position—it proves that institutional practice and honesty are not compatible.

BELLMAN. Why do you say that?
JIM. We should be treated as individuals, but we're handled in categories—the same routine for everyone. What is it, Doctor—inexperience? Lack of time?
BELLMAN. I can't discuss that with you, Mr. Downs.
JIM. That woman wound up in the violent ward for her pains. What will happen to me?
BELLMAN. We'll see. Stand up, Mr. Downs. (JIM *does so*.) Hold your arms out with your fingers extended. All right—now close your eyes. (JIM *stands that way for nearly a minute.* BELLMAN *rises, crosses to in front of desk, watches* JIM *carefully, then crosses back of desk again.*) All right. Now look at my finger. (*Moves his finger from* L. *to* R. *several times, in same pattern as* SCHLESINGER.) All right. That's all for now.
JIM. When do I go home?
BELLMAN. (*Firmly.*) You don't, Mr. Downs. Not for a while.

LIGHTS FADE QUICKLY

## ACT II

### Scene 3

SCENE: *The ward. Screen has been returned to its position, desk and two chairs of previous scene removed.*

TIME: *Close to 9 P. M., the same day.*

*It is near bedtime. Those who were in street clothes have changed to pajamas.*

CARLISLE *fusses with his bed, mumbling quietly to himself.* SCHLOSS *is sitting up and writing, using his drawn-up knees as a desk.*

JIM *is sitting on his bed.* ANKORITIS *is standing* R. *of* JIM. TAGER *is sitting on his bed facing* JIM. O'BRIEN *and* MAJOR *are sitting on* TAGER'S *bed,* O'BRIEN *downstage,* TAGER *in the middle.* MAJOR, *upstage.*

TAGER. The theater must be a fascinating business, Mr. Downs.
O'BRIEN. Who do you know, Mr. Downs—any movie stars?
ANKORITIS. Of course, the theater originated in Greece.

TAGER. It did, Mr. Downs?
ANKORITIS. Everybody knows that.
TAGER. (*To* JIM.) Is that right, Mr. Downs?
ANKORITIS. (*Offended.*) You question my veracity?
TAGER. If Mr. Downs says so, it's all right. He's a professional ——
(MISS WINGATE *enters ward from* L. *She is tall, heavy, middle-aged, unintelligent, and has the broadest possible southern accent.*)
MISS WINGATE. (*As she goes to her desk—which is* HANSEN'S *desk—with a small bottle of medicine.*) Bed-time, boys. Nine o'clock.
O'BRIEN. (*To* JIM—*eagerly.*) Do you know any movie stars?
JIM. I've met a few.
MISS WINGATE. (*As she crosses to* R. *of* SCHLOSS'S *bed.*) Get to bed, boys. It's nine o'clock. Light's going out. I can't stand here all night—I've got work to do. (*Group breaks up, everyone gets into bed.* O'BRIEN *remains on* TAGER'S *bed.*)
O'BRIEN. Who do you know?
MISS WINGATE. (*Turns to* O'BRIEN.) O'Brien, your bed's not over there. Now get into bed.
O'BRIEN. Yes, Miss Wingate. (*Scurries back to his own bed.*)
MISS WINGATE. Now I don't want to hear any noise from this ward. You boys keep the whole floor awake with your noise at night, (*Turns* R. *and exits as she speaks.*) and I'm not going to stand for any more noise—do you hear?
O'BRIEN. Good night, Miss Wingate.
MISS WINGATE. (*Returns to just* R. *of* O'BRIEN'S *bed.*) Don't you tell me good night?
ANKORITIS. Good night, Miss Wingate.
MISS WINGATE. (*Crosses to front of* TAGER'S *bed.*) Who was that—Ankoritis?
ANKORITIS. Yes, Miss Wingate—and it's pronounced Ankoreetis. It is a name, not a disease.
MISS WINGATE. (*Furious.*) Is that so? (*Crosses up to* ANKORITIS' *bed*—R. *side.*) Well, you'd just better be careful how you talk to me, Ankoritis, or you'll wind up in Seven—and I don't think you'd like that.
TAGER. Would you put the lights out, please, Miss Wingate? I want to get to sleep.
MISS WINGATE. (*Turns to* TAGER.) You *get* to sleep, Mr. Tager, and I'll put the lights out when I get good and ready. (*As she crosses down to light switch, which is on upstage panel of door frame.*) You boys think you're smart. The whole lot of you will wind up in Seven if you're not

careful. (*Turns to men as she takes key for light switch from her pocket.*) Seventy-two patients in this ward, and you men are the worst.
O'BRIEN. Good night, Miss Wingate.
ANKORITIS. May your repose in the arms of Morpheus be a pleasant one, Miss Wingate.
MISS WINGATE. Thank you. Good night. (*She goes out* L., *after putting out ward lights with a key.*)
O'BRIEN. (*Kneels on his bed, facing* JIM—*calls softly.*) Mr. Downs—what movie stars do you know?
JIM. (*Quietly.*) I'll tell you tomorrow. (*Pause.* O'BRIEN *lies down again.*)
CARLISLE. Well—another day—another dollar. (*Pause.*)
MAJOR. (*Quietly, from his bed.*) You can make up the dollar—but you can't make up the day. In this place—it's just gone. (*Pause.*)
O'BRIEN. (*Softly—raises himself on his elbow—to* JIM.) Do you know Betty Grable?
SCHLOSS. (*In a tense whisper.*) Shut up, for Christ's sake! You ever got near Betty Grable you'd wet your pants.
O'BRIEN. (*Just as tense a whisper.*) Is that so?
SCHLOSS. Yeah—that's so.
O'BRIEN. In Havana one time I saw ——
SCHLOSS. In Havana your mother was a whore ——
O'BRIEN. (*His emotion overcoming him, though the voice is not loud.*) I'll break your neck!
SCHLOSS. (*Waits just a second to seize his advantage.*) You threatened me! (*Suddenly yells.*) Miss Wingate! (*Throws covers off, jumps out of bed,* R. *side.*) Miss Wingate! (*Crosses down to front of his bed. Others sit up in their beds.*) Miss Wingate!
TAGER. Keep your mouth shut, Mr. Schloss!
MAJOR. Aw, forget it, Mr. Schloss.
CARLISLE. Leave him alone. (MISS WINGATE *appears from* L., *above door. Crosses behind her desk to* L. *of* JIM'S *bed.*) } (*Together.*)
SCHLOSS. He threatened me, Miss Wingate.
MISS WINGATE. Who?
SCHLOSS. Mr. O'Brien. He said he'd break my neck.
MISS WINGATE. He did? (*A few steps toward* C.) O'Brien, did you say you were going to break Mr. Schloss's neck? O'Brien, are you in your bed? (*As she turns, crosses* R. *to light switch, puts lights on.*) Well, I'll soon find out. (*Crosses back to* U. L. *of* O'BRIEN'S *bed.* O'BRIEN *is kneeling on floor,* R. *of his bed, hysterical with fear.*) Did you hear

me talking to you, Mr. O'Brien? You know what happens to people who make threats down here? (*All the men are watching in helpless rage.* SCHLOSS *is* U. L. *of his bed.*) Mr. Schloss, get the attendants—I'll call the doctor in a minute. (SCHLOSS *goes off* R.)

TAGER. (*Gets out of bed,* R. *side.*) Miss Wingate—Mr. Schloss ——

MISS WINGATE. (*Turns to him.*) I don't want to hear a word out of any of you. (*Turns back to* O'BRIEN.) No point asking you, O'Brien, whether you threatened Mr. Schloss—of course you'll deny it.

O'BRIEN. (*Through wild sobbing.*) He—he—said my mother—he—insulted my mother ——

MISS WINGATE. I don't care what he said about your mother—you can't go around threatening people. When you get to Seven you won't be able to threaten anybody. (TWO ATTENDANTS *enter from* R.) Here he is—take him up. I'll call the doctor.

O'BRIEN. (*Backs away from them on his knees, crying.*) Don't take me to Seven—please don't take me to Seven! (ATTENDANTS *take his arms.* WINGATE *crosses ahead of them to door, opens it and holds it open as they drag* O'BRIEN, *struggling and screaming through door* L.) Please don't take me to Seven! Please don't take me to Seven!

MISS WINGATE. (*Locks door, puts out lights, turns to men.*) Now all you men get back to sleep. I don't want to hear another word, d'you hear? Get to sleep, all of you. (*As she goes to desk, sits.*) Land a'mercy, I don't know how I'm going to get my work done with all this going on. (SCHLOSS *enters* R., *goes to his bed.*) Oh, Mr. Downs—you asleep?

JIM. (*From his bed.*) No.

MISS WINGATE. (*Takes telegram from her pocket.*) There's a telegram for you. Been here for a while, but I've just been so busy I haven't had time to even think about it.

JIM. (*Still shocked by what has happened.*) Thank you, Miss Wingate.

MISS WINGATE. (*After pause.*) Well, don't you want it?

JIM. (*Slowly.*) Yes—yes, of course. (*Gets out of bed, goes to her.*)

MISS WINGATE. Here it is. (*She hands him telegram.*) You can read it at the desk. You'll have to show it to me when you're finished.

JIM. (*Stands* R. *of* WINGATE, *takes telegram, holds it a moment.*) Miss Wingate—that O'Brien boy ——

MISS WINGATE. Never mind about that O'Brien boy. What does the telegram say? (JIM *reads telegram, then hands it to* MISS WINGATE. *She reads it aloud.*) "Darling, you must tell doctors you want to see me—otherwise am not permitted—I love you—Charlotte." Well, who's this Charlotte?

JIM. Isn't it plain enough?
MISS WINGATE. But you have a wife, haven't you?
JIM. (*Exasperated.*) We were separated, Miss Wingate—for three months, before this happened.
MISS WINGATE. Well, I don't care how long you're separated—you're still married, aren't you?
JIM. Yes.
MISS WINGATE. You have a wife and a girl friend?
JIM. That's hardly the way to put it ——
MISS WINGATE. I don't care how you put it. Have you seen this girl since you've been here?
JIM. You saw the telegram.
MISS WINGATE. Well, my advice to you is to write this girl tonight ——
JIM. But ——
MISS WINGATE. No buts, Mr. Downs. I'm trying to help you. The law recognizes only the wife—so get used to it. What are you trying to do—break down the sanctity of marriage?
JIM. Miss Wingate, I ——
MISS WINGATE. Your wife can get you out of here if she wants to.
JIM. (*His thought arrested.*) She can?
MISS WINGATE. We can't hold you, Mr. Downs, if she wants to take you home.
JIM. You sure about that?
MISS WINGATE. Of course I'm sure. That's the law. It happens all the time. So if I were you I would tell this girl you don't want to see her again. I'll give you paper and pencil. Here—you write it right now and I'll mail it for you.
JIM. (*Takes paper and pencil.*) Suppose I just say, "Don't try to see me—I'll explain when I get out."
MISS WINGATE. (*Thinks about it.*) Well—what happens outside is none of my business—I guess it's all right.
JIM. Thank you. (*Starts to write, then stops.*) Miss Wingate—that O'Brien boy really didn't do anything ——
MISS WINGATE. Now, Mr. Downs—you keep *your* nose clean.
JIM. But is it possible—without proof—without knowing who's right or who's wrong—to ——?
MISS WINGATE. I'm trying to help you, Mr. Downs. Just you write your little note and stay out of anybody else's business. You got your own problems to worry about.
JIM. (*Looks at her, finishes note, gives it to her.*) Thank you, Miss

Wingate. (*Goes back to his bed. A moment's pause, then very quietly* CARLISLE *gets out of his bed.*)
CARLISLE. (*Gently shakes front of* TAGER'S *bed.*) Come on, boys, get up. (*Goes to* JIM'S *bed.*) My daughter's comin' home—she won't like it, she catch you here. (*Shakes* ANKORITIS' *bed.*) Now, come on, boys—please. Get your clothes on and go home. My daughter won't like it at all, she find you here. (*Goes to* MISS WINGATE.) Time for these boys to be gettin' on home—my daughter ——
MISS WINGATE. (*Takes* CARLISLE *by arm—her voice is soft—it can be on occasion—as she walks him back to his bed.*) Now you go to bed, Mr. Carlisle—I'll take care of your daughter when she comes.
CARLISLE. (*Always gentle.*) You will? Thank you. (*Peacefully, gets into bed.*) My daughter's very funny that way. Good night, Miss Wingate.
MISS WINGATE. (*Quietly, as she fixes his covers.*) Good night, Mr. Carlisle. (*She crosses* L. *as* ——)

## LIGHTS FADE QUICKLY

## ACT II

### SCENE 4

SCENE: *The same.*

TIME: *The next day, Thursday, 2 P. M.*

*As lights come up bell at door is heard.* JIM *is alone, sitting on his bed.* GREGORY *crosses stage from* R. *to* L., *unlocks door.* ANN *is there.*

GREGORY. These aren't visiting hours.
ANN. (*Handing him pass.*) I have a special pass.
GREGORY. (*Looks at it, then at* ANN.) I'll have to examine your package.
ANN. Certainly. (*Gives him package of fruit.*)
GREGORY. (*After examining package.*) O.K. (*Lets her pass, locks door, then goes off* R. JIM *has risen, comes down to* R. *side of his bed.*)
ANN. (*Goes to* L. *side of* JIM'S *bed.*) Jim . . .
JIM. (*Has watched what happened—he is waiting.*) Ann ——
ANN. Well—you look fine. Much better than you did upstairs.
JIM. Hm-hmmmn.

ANN. I brought you some fruit, and some chocolate.
JIM. (*Takes package, crosses up to cabinet, R. side of his bed.*) Thanks, Ann. I was going to ask you. Most of the fellows pretty much share what they get.
ANN. (*Crosses up L. side of* JIM'S *bed, takes off her coat, puts it on* ANKORITIS' *bed.*) I'll bring more next time.
JIM. I'm hoping there won't be a next time.
ANN. (*Takes her purse, sits on* JIM'S *bed, facing him.*) What did your new doctor say?
JIM. (*A few steps down to her.*) Do you know him?
ANN. I haven't met him—I've spoken to him on the phone. He sounds nice.
JIM. He said I'd have to stay awhile. Ann, I want to get out of here.
ANN. Of course, dear. I'm doing everything I can.
JIM. (*Sits on* TAGER'S *bed, facing* ANN.) You can get me out on your say-so. You can do it, Ann—if you want to.
ANN. Of course I want to. But it isn't as simple as all that.
JIM. (*Urgently.*) It is, Ann. I've learned that. The night nurse told me.
ANN. Well, I don't know what she told you, but I spoke to Dr. Bellman this morning on the phone, and he said you'll have to stay awhile.
JIM. (*Rises—stares at her—a brief pause.*) Ann—are you trying to have me committed?
ANN. That's silly, dear. You're upset. I can understand that.
JIM. (*Becoming more and more agitated—crosses to head of his bed, turns to her.*) No, you can't understand. *I* am the one behind locked doors, not you. You can come and go as you like. Every day I stand at the barred window and hear those boat whistles and automobile horns, and the sounds spell freedom, but I'm not free.
ANN. You will be, dear.
JIM. (*Crosses down to her.*) Don't pretty it up, Ann. You don't know what goes on here. (*Sits on* TAGER'S *bed again, facing* ANN.) I've seen fears built up in these men that didn't exist before. I don't know why most of them are here, but after they spend a day in this place, those fears take over.
ANN. How do you know that?
JIM. I know, because it's happening to me. I want to go home, Ann.
ANN. What sort of fears?
JIM. (*Almost angrily.*) Seven—and the green slip. You should hear the men talking about them.
ANN. They must be hospital terms—what do they mean?

JIM. Seven is the violent ward and the green slip is commitment to a State Hospital.
ANN. Well, that's not going to happen to you.
JIM. It can. It can. I've seen it happen on the flimsiest pretext. You've got to hold on tight to keep your balance here, Ann. Everything you say and do is reported. You are constantly watched. I shouldn't even be getting so excited now. If I'm seen, it will set me back God knows how long. You can't have normal feelings here, Ann. Only continuous calm. Is that normal—for anyone?
ANN. You're exaggerating, dear.
JIM. (*Near the end of his rope.*) Exaggerating? (*Starts to cry.*) My God, how can I make you understand? (*Rises, crosses R. to front of* SCHLOSS' *bed.*)
ANN. I tell you you're not being committed.
JIM. (*Turns to* ANN.) How do you know?
ANN. I had a long talk with Dr. Davidson——
JIM. (*Crosses back to R. of his bed.*) Davidson! What did you go to see him about?
ANN. I think you'll be pleased. I thought if our own doctor—he's known the two of us for eight years or more—would intercede——
JIM. (*Impatiently—as he sits on* TAGER'S *bed again.*) Fine—fine! What's he going to do?
ANN. He has some influence with the Veterans' Administration, and he thought maybe he could get you into a Veterans' Hospital.
JIM. (*Almost shouts, rising.*) No! I want to go home!
ANN. (*Quietly.*) Hush, Jim.
JIM. (*Voice lower, but still intense, crosses a few steps to R.*) I don't want any hospital. I want to go home. (*Turns back to* ANN.) I'm not a mental case. Do you think I'm a mental case?
ANN. No, Jim—of course not. But Davidson thought you might need psychiatric help—after what you did.
JIM. (*Turns away from her, a few steps to R.*) What I did is over—I'm alive now. I'm no more ill than you are. (*Stops, cries helplessly.*) But I don't seem able to convince anybody. (*The briefest pause—turns to* ANN.) Ann, why did you tell Dr. Bellman I was belligerent and nasty?
ANN. Why did I what?
JIM. (*Crosses slowly back to her.*) Was I ever belligerent to you?
ANN. No, dear.
JIM. And you told him that at times I was wild and incoherent.

ANN. I don't know why he would tell you those things, Jim, I ——
JIM. (*Has reached* R. *side of his bed.*) How are you helping me, Ann, if you tell the doctor I'm belligerent and nasty—and wild and incoherent?
ANN. You don't give me a chance to explain.
JIM. (*Stands over her,* R. *side of his bed.*) What can you say? I hardly think he made it up.
ANN. When you say things like that, I think Davidson's right.
JIM. (*Quickly.*) Then you *do* think I'm sick?
ANN. I didn't say that.
JIM. (*Crosses to* L. *of* ANN, *as he keeps his eyes on her all the time.*) Ann, I warn you—if I get a green slip, I'll fight it. I'll fight it in court. You're allowed to, you know—the court sits right here in this building.
ANN. You don't have to fight me!
JIM. (*His emotion mounting.*) Then why aren't you trying to get me out, instead of talking about my going to another hospital?
ANN. We thought it was best ——
JIM. If I need help, I can get it outside.
ANN. We can't afford it, Jim. Private psychiatrists are so expensive.
JIM. (*This is the peak of his emotion.*) I can go to a clinic—I can go to the V.A., but I'll be free—I'll be home—I won't be confined in an institution. (*A pause—he quiets down.*) I lie awake at night—and they know it because they walk through the ward three or four times a night with a flashlight. If you sleep, that's good—if you don't sleep, that's a sign of nervousness. Last night, I pretended to sleep, and this morning the nurse said, "I'm glad you're feeling better, Mr. Downs." (*Leans on* WINGATE'S *desk.*)
ANN. (*Pause—quietly.*) What do you want me to do?
JIM. (*Helplessly—crosses to front of* TAGER'S *bed.*) I had thought of reaching Davidson myself, but now it turns out he thinks I belong here ——
ANN. He doesn't think that—he thinks you need help.
JIM. (*Urgently—turns to her, sits once more* L. *side of* TAGER'S *bed.*) Then tell him to come down here, and see Dr. Bellman. And get Dr. Walker—he's a psychiatrist, he knows the routine—he's the one who wanted me to write a play with him. They've got to come down here—just phoning the hospital is not enough. Tell them I'll pay them for their time, if that's necessary. I'll get the money some way. But they've got to come down here—tomorrow.
ANN. All right, I'll call them.

JIM. (*His tears give way.*) You can't just ask them, Please, will you do it? You've got to make them see how important it is.
ANN. I will. I will, dear. (BELLMAN *enters from* R., *crosses to* R. *of* TAGER'S *bed.*)
BELLMAN. Is this your wife, Mr. Downs?
JIM. (*Turns upstage, away from* BELLMAN, *to hide his tears.*) Yes. Ann, this is Dr. Bellman.
ANN. How do you do?
BELLMAN. I'd like to see you for a minute, Mrs. Downs.
ANN. (*Gets up.*) Certainly.
BELLMAN. No, take your time. When you've spoken to your husband. (*To* JIM.) How do you feel?
JIM. (*Mutters, still facing upstage.*) Fine. (BELLMAN *crosses to desk* D. L., *sits.* JIM *comes down to front of* TAGER'S *bed.*) Maybe you'd better speak to him now.
ANN. In a minute—he's busy now. Jim—is it true you tried to reach Charlotte?
JIM. (*Stunned.*) Why?
ANN. Now don't pretend. Dr. Schlesinger told me.
JIM. (*In a trap.*) Is—is that so unnatural?
ANN. (*That awful bravery.*) No. I just wanted to know how you felt.
JIM. Well, Ann, it's no secret that ——
ANN. It's also no secret that I've done a great deal for you since you came to the hospital.
JIM. I know, Ann. Everyone's told me.
ANN. Oh, before I forget. Would you endorse this for me? (*Takes check from her purse.*)
JIM. What's this?
ANN. The check for your teaching. Endorse it to me. (*Takes fountain pen from purse, opens it.*)
JIM. But I won't have a nickel when I get out of the hospital.
ANN. I'm not asking anything for myself. There are bills to pay . . . money for the special nurses, and God knows what else—they're all your expenses. (*Hands* JIM *pen and check.*)
JIM. (*Helplessly—taking them.*) Yes, Ann.
ANN. (*Closes purse, offers it to* JIM *to write on. She continues to hold purse.*) Here. (JIM *endorses check, hands it and pen to* ANN. ANN *puts pen and check in purse.*) I'd better see Dr. Bellman now.
JIM. (*Turns away from* ANN, *to* R.) Yes.
ANN. (*Puts purse on* JIM'S *bed, gets coat, puts it on.*) Oh, I spoke to

Mr. Williams for you. It's too bad you couldn't make that appointment. He had just about settled on you for the job.
JIM. (*Dumbly.*) He had?
ANN. (*Comes down to foot of bed, picks up purse.*) That should make you feel *good*—to know that he wanted you.
JIM. Yes, it does.
ANN. I'd better see Dr. Bellman now. (*She takes a few steps to* JIM.) I'll see you Saturday. Take care, dear. (*Turns, starts* L., *to* BELLMAN.)
JIM. Thanks. Oh, Ann —— (*A step to her.*) You have my keys?
ANN. (*Has stopped, turns to* JIM.) Yes.
JIM. Bring some clothes for me, will you? These things —— (*He fingers the pajamas.*)
ANN. Of course—Saturday. (*Starts for* BELLMAN.)
JIM. (*Turns, calls again to* ANN.) Ann ——
ANN. (*Stops, crosses* R. *to him.*) Yes?
JIM. (*Leads her* R. *a step.*) Ask Dr. Bellman whether *you* can get me out on your own, will you?
ANN. Of course.
JIM. You won't forget?
ANN. No, dear. (JIM *goes silently off* R. ANN *crosses to* R. *of* BELLMAN.) Dr. Bellman?
BELLMAN. (*Gets up from desk.*) Mrs. Downs.
ANN. They certainly keep you busy.
BELLMAN. (*Attempting to smile.*) Well—I wish I could spend more time with the men's families. I could learn a lot more about the men themselves. But —— (*Shrugs shoulders.*)
ANN. I understand.
BELLMAN. What do you *think*?
ANN. About Jim? He frightens me—the things he says.
BELLMAN. He shows quite a bit of antagonism and resentment. I don't think he's telling the complete truth yet. There are many questions he refuses to answer.
ANN. Dr. Bellman—he's afraid of being committed.
BELLMAN. (*Alert.*) Did he say that?
ANN. Yes. Is it possible he may be committed?
BELLMAN. There are several possibilities, Mrs. Downs. He can be discharged in your custody—if you want to assume that responsibility.
ANN. I'd gladly assume that responsibility, Doctor—but if he isn't well enough?
BELLMAN. He may be committed to a State Hospital.

ANN. I see. He wants me to reach several doctor friends on the outside—what do you think?
BELLMAN. I wouldn't suggest it.
ANN. You know best, Doctor. Thank you.
BELLMAN. Not at all. Now if you'll forgive me? (*Crosses* L. *to open door for* ANN.)
ANN. Certainly. (*Starts for door as* ——)

## LIGHTS FADE QUICKLY

## ACT II

### SCENE 5

SCENE: *The same.*

TIME: *Five days later, Tuesday.*

MAJOR *is singing a calypso song and drumming its rhythm on* HANSEN'S *desk, which has been shifted slightly on stage, and angled so that* MAJOR *faces* D. L. *corner.* ANKORITIS *is seated opposite him on downstage side of table.* TAGER *is standing between them. All three are singing, though* MAJOR *is the expert. They are having fun.* JIM *is sitting alone, on his bed, facing* R. SCHLOSS *is sitting on his bed, writing.* CARLISLE *is asleep in his bed, down* R.

TAGER. (*After a moment of singing.*) Come over here, Mr. Downs. You'll like this.
MISS WINGATE. (*Enters* R., *goes to* CARLISLE'S *bed.*) Time for your medicine, Mr. Carlisle. (WINGATE *pulls cover off* CARLISLE, *he pulls it back again.* WINGATE *throws cover off.*)
JIM. (*Looks up—sees* WINGATE.) Miss Wingate ——
MISS WINGATE. (*Helping* CARLISLE *out of bed.*) I'm busy.
JIM. (*Goes to her.*) Can I have ——? (*Turns to men drumming and singing.*) Please—fellows—hold it down—hold it down —— (*Men look at him strangely, soften their singing.* JIM *turns back to* WINGATE.) Can I have an appointment with Dr. Bellman?
MISS WINGATE. (*Getting* CARLISLE *out of bed.*) You had your interview with him, didn't you?
JIM. Yes.

MISS WINGATE. (*As she exits off* R., *with* CARLISLE.) He'll call you if he wants to talk to you again.
JIM. But I want to —— (MISS WINGATE *leaves with* CARLISLE. JIM *is left standing. The volume of drumming and singing increases, he turns to men, bothered by noise—then starts for his bed.*)
GREGORY. (*Enters* L., *starts collecting dominoes, checkers, magazines, etc. from beds* No. 6, No. 5, *and* No. 3.) You fellows are not supposed to take these games out of the day room—you know that.
JIM. (*As* GREGORY *is at bed* No. 3, JIM *turns to him.*) Don ——
GREGORY. Sloppiest bunch of guys I ever saw.
JIM. (*Goes to him, he cannot stand much more of the noise and, as he talks, keeps turning to men.*) Don—do I get another appointment with Bellman?
GREGORY. He'll call you, Jim. Have you had any tests?
JIM. I took the Rorschach yesterday.
GREGORY. It'll take at least a week for the results of that to come through.
JIM. (*Finally shouts at men, violently.*) For God's sake, fellows—you're not the only ones in this ward! (*Starts* L., *toward men.*)
GREGORY. (*Goes to him.*) Take it easy, Jim.
JIM. (*Looks at him savagely*—GREGORY *seems no longer his friend.*) You, too. Take it easy. Take it easy. (JIM *turns away.*)
GREGORY. (*Takes* JIM'S *arm.*) Lie down awhile, Jim. Try to relax. (JIM *wrenches away—goes to the drumming group—suddenly throws table over with his hands. Men jump from their chairs, and fall back startled.* GREGORY *grabs* JIM, *pinning his arms, turning him around.*) What do you think you're doing? Do you know what would happen if I reported this?
JIM. (*Still struggling.*) Report it! Go ahead and report it! I don't want any favors. (*Breaks away from* GREGORY *again, starts* R., *but* GREGORY *grabs him almost immediately.*)
GREGORY. (*Shouts.*) Jim! (*Tightens his grip on* JIM'S *arm*—JIM *quiets down.*) Come here, Jim. Sit down. (*Takes him to his bed, seats him at foot of bed, and sits on* ANKORITIS' *bed, facing him.*)
JIM. (*Almost crying.*) Why are they keeping me? What have I done? I hurt no one but myself. Until I took the pills nobody questioned me. Nobody stopped me on the street as if I were a suspicious character. Well—I'm still the same guy. What's the difference now?
GREGORY. The difference is that you *took* the pills.
JIM. But ——

GREGORY. What's the difference between a guy just holding a gun and a guy that pulls the trigger? The fact that he did it ——
JIM. (*Holds his head.*) Christ, Don—I don't want any riddles! Why are they keeping me?
GREGORY. (*Kneels to him—patiently.*) Listen to me, Jim. The doctors take most cases of suicide to be an inverted homicidal tendency. Do you know what that means? (JIM *raises head, looks at* GREGORY. GREGORY *explains.*) You're a potential murderer in their eyes—even though you only tried to kill yourself. (JIM *looks wordlessly at* GREGORY. GREGORY *stands up, pats him gently on shoulder—crosses to bed No. 3, picks up games and magazines he placed there when* JIM *started for men, crosses to group at table. He turns back to look at* JIM—*then nods to group.*) O.K., fellows. But take it easy. (*Goes off L. Men in the group look at* JIM. MAJOR *starts another calypso song quietly. Soon the tempo is increasing—others join in. The volume swells, and men are no longer looking at* JIM. *He sits forlornly, looking at them. Slowly, he turns to window. Gets up from the bed, takes step to window, and his head falls pathetically to one side, as he looks up at window, his back to audience. The drumming and singing have reached a crescendo.*)

## CURTAIN

## ACT III

### Scene 1

SCENE: *The dining-room. It is essentially the same set—the windows and door remain where they were. But beds have been removed, and tables and chairs are in their place. There are four oblong tables, numbered from* R. *to* L., *No. 1, No. 2, No. 3, No. 4. Ordinary bent-wood chairs on either side of each table. Only* MISS HANSEN'S *desk remains in its original position throughout the play.*

*It is visiting day, but early.*

GREGORY *is unlocking door.* ANN *and* HARRY DOWNS, JIM'S *brother, take a step inside. He is a small-town businessman.*

ANN. Show him your pass, Harry. (*To* GREGORY.) This is Mr. Downs' brother. (ANN *crosses* R. *to* C.)
GREGORY. (*Takes pass from* DOWNS, *reads it carefully—then looks at him briefly.*) Will you have a seat? (*Turns to* ANN.) I'll call him.
ANN. Thank you. (GREGORY *goes off* R. *It is obvious that* DOWNS *is aware of the place he is in. Moves as though he were afraid to do the wrong thing. Crosses slowly to* L. *of* ANN.) This is the dining-room.
DOWNS. (*Looking round, nods head.*) Hm-hmmm.
ANN. (*Making conversation.*) He forgot to look in my package. They examine everything before they let you in.
DOWNS. (*As he crosses to* R. *of* ANN.) Do you see all kinds—I mean, the violent ones, too?
ANN. No. They're on a different floor. This is only the observation ward.
DOWNS. (*Turns to* ANN.) Why was he sent here?
ANN. (*Disturbed, looks at* DOWNS.) You know what he did.
DOWNS. I know—but hundreds of people have tried the same thing. They don't wind up in a—in a —— (*Almost afraid to name the place.*)
ANN. (*Quickly.*) This isn't that kind of place, really. (JIM *enters* R. *He hasn't slept and his eyes show it. He seems almost as uncertain as he did when he first came to "One," even though his attitude is now*

*quietly cynical. He sees* DOWNS, *stops—a strange embarrassment comes over him at the realization of where they are meeting.* ANN *takes a step down-stage when* JIM *enters,* DOWNS *turns to face* JIM.)
JIM. (*Quietly.*) Hello, Harry.
DOWNS. How do you feel? (L. *of* JIM.)
JIM. All right. When did you get here?
DOWNS. I flew in from Pittsburgh this morning. I had a few errands to do when I got to the city—then I called Ann.
JIM. (*To* DOWNS.) Why did it take you so long to get here?
DOWNS. What do you mean?
JIM. I've been here two weeks and you're just getting around to visit me.
DOWNS. I'm not a free man, Jim. I've got things to do.
JIM. More important things, of course.
DOWNS. I'm sorry, Jim. I just couldn't ——
JIM. Yeah —— (*Bitterly.*) Well—how do you like the place?
DOWNS. How long will they keep you here?
JIM. I don't know.
DOWNS. I was wondering if I could visit with your doctor a few minutes ——?
JIM. What for?
DOWNS. Just to talk to him. Do you suppose he's in?
JIM. (*Indicates off* R., *with his head.*) The office is down the hall, on your right. Ask for Dr. Bellman.
DOWNS. (*To* ANN.) Excuse me. (*Goes off down* R.)
ANN. (*Puts package she brought for* JIM *on table No. 3.*) Why were you so mean to Harry?
JIM. You'd think he'd take a little more interest in his brother.
ANN. Some of your students called—they heard you were sick.
JIM. How did they know to call you?
ANN. (*Hesitantly.*) I had your phone disconnected and the calls switched to me.
JIM. Well, that's fine. I'll only have to connect it again, that's all.
ANN. The company would have taken it out anyway—there was no one to pay the bill. You can't go back to that cold water flat, Jim. The doctors say it would be too depressing.
JIM. They didn't say that to me.
ANN. Dr. Bellman—Dr. Schlesinger—they all said it.
JIM. To you?
ANN. Yes.

JIM. It's nice of them to be so concerned. Are *they* going to find me an apartment?
ANN. We'll manage, dear—don't worry.
JIM. I see. (*Brief pause.*) Do my students know what happened?
ANN. No. I wasn't sure what to tell them. They all want to visit you—I had quite a time putting them off. I said you were in the hospital for tests—it's vague enough. They say what kind of tests, and I tell them I really don't know.
JIM. They must think it's awfully mysterious. Well, I'll reach them when I get out. (*Sits* R. *of table No. 2.*)
ANN. Jim—I—I had to tell them not to wait for you—to go ahead and find another teacher.
JIM. (*Turns on her quickly—his tone is sharp.*) Why?
ANN. I had to, Jim. Dr. Bellman said it might be some time. I had to say there was no way of knowing how long you'd be sick, and it was better not to wait.
JIM. (*Looks at her briefly.*) I see.
ANN. (*An attempt at brightness.*) Everyone's been calling about you. (*Sits* L. *of table No. 3.*)
JIM. That's great. Did you reach Davidson and Walker?
ANN. I called them, Jim—really I did. Dr. Walker said he couldn't take the responsibility. And you *know* how Davidson feels.
JIM. (*Disillusioned—angry.*) I see. Well, it seems that the people I counted on to say I'm well are the very ones who now say I'm sick.
ANN. Why do you say that?
JIM. (*Losing his temper briefly.*) I'm still here—that's why I say it.
ANN. We're doing everything we can . . .
JIM. (*More quietly, but still bitter.*) I know, Ann, I know. I know, I know —— (DOWNS *returns to* R. *of table No. 2.* JIM *turns to him.*) What did he say?
DOWNS. I only spoke to him for a minute.
JIM. So?
DOWNS. (*Disturbed.*) Apparently, Jim, you've said and done things since you've been here—that give them the right to have doubts about you.
JIM. What did I say?
DOWNS. I don't know—he wouldn't tell *me,* of course, but ——
ANN. Dr. Bellman did tell me you showed a great deal of antagonism and resentment ——
JIM. What do they expect, for God's sake? They probe and pry and

get you upset—and then expect you to behave like a normal human being.

DOWNS. They're the bosses here, Jim.

JIM. But they don't even tell me what I'm here for.

ANN. You should try to cooperate, dear. Dr. Bellman said there were many questions you refused to answer.

JIM. It's none of their business.

ANN. But it is, Jim. They only want to help you. You should tell them everything.

JIM. Do you know they think I'm a potential murderer?

ANN. That's ridiculous, Jim.

JIM. The attendant told me.

ANN. And you listened to *him*?

JIM. It's logical, isn't it? They feel I've turned my hostility against myself.

DOWNS. Jim—listen to *me!*

ANN. (*Almost on top of* DOWNS' *line.*) Tell them everything, Jim—and tell them the truth.

JIM. (*With impatience and strength.*) But I have—I haven't lied about a thing. Everything I said—to Schlesinger—to Bellman—to the nurses—to the psychologist who gave me the Rorschach test—to anyone here—has been the truth.

DOWNS. Ann—may I speak to Jim alone, please?

ANN. What can you have to say that I mustn't hear?

DOWNS. Ann—after all—what's wrong with wanting to speak to my brother?

ANN. (*Suddenly, she is the injured one.*) Why am I in the way?

DOWNS. Ann, it's nearly two o'clock—people will be coming in. Give me a few minutes with Jim alone.

ANN. Where can I go? I'm not allowed anywhere but here.

JIM. (*Rises, crosses impatiently to* L. *of* ANN.) Go to the office—ask one of the nurses—go out for coffee—anything. (ANN *puts handkerchief to her mouth.*) Ann, don't start crying. (ANN *rises, goes off down* R. JIM *turns away, irritably, takes few steps to* C.) Well, go ahead and talk—what did you want to tell me?

DOWNS. (*Drops his hat on table No. 2, but still wears his overcoat. Crosses down to* R. *of* JIM.) First—you've got to stop shooting off your mouth. Now listen to me for a change—I've got something I want to tell you. From the minute I learned you were in this place, I've been worried. Back home I asked around quietly—a doctor friend, a lawyer

friend—I had to be careful. You know what Keysport is like—if it got out I had a brother in an ——
JIM. Insane asylum.
DOWNS. (*Apologizing.*) Well—you know, Jim—it sounds awful. There's Helen and the children—and it just isn't good for my business.
JIM. (*Turns to* DOWNS.) So?
DOWNS. They couldn't advise me, Jim—they said the law in this state may be different from ours. But they gave me the names of a couple of people to see ——
JIM. Did you talk to them?
DOWNS. Yes—this morning.
JIM. And?
DOWNS. They can't do a thing. (JIM *crosses up to* R. *of table No. 4.*) You're in the hands of the authorities now. (DOWNS *follows to table No. 3. He sits on* L. *corner of table No. 3.*) The police picked you up—and a City hospital has you in custody. (JIM *sits* R. *of table No. 4.*) If you want to get out of here—you've got to play ball.
JIM. How?
DOWNS. In two ways. First, as far as the hospital is concerned. (*Gets off table, takes step down-stage, looks off* R., *then turns back to* JIM.) You know how to handle a cop, don't you?
JIM. How do you mean?
DOWNS. (*Returns to sitting on* L. *corner of table No. 3.*) Jim—I have never paid a fine in my life. Because I know that I never know more than a cop. *He's* the smart one—not me. And it's "Yes, officer," and "No, officer" and "I'm sorry, sir." Don't try to know more than these people. If you want to get out of here, you'll *have to swallow everything.* (JIM *turns away resentfully, making a smothered sound of "Augh."*) Well—what's being proud going to get you? Don't *I* have to compromise every day of my life? I've got a lousy insurance business, so I get drunk with a client, watch him make passes at Helen—and flatter the hell out of him. Do you think I like it? (JIM *looks at him.* DOWNS *continues meaningfully.*) It's no different in here. It's no different out there. Try it. What can you lose?
JIM. (*Slowly, after a brief pause.*) A model patient?
DOWNS. Try it.
JIM. (*Another pause—quietly—we see he is considering the idea.*) What else?
DOWNS. (*Puts foot on chair in front of him.*) With Ann it will be

harder. I don't know how things were with you in the past few years—you seldom wrote. But you were separated—is that right?
JIM. Yes.
DOWNS. I went down to that address you gave me in the letter—your apartment's been rented to somebody else.
JIM. (*Stunned.*) And all my things?
DOWNS. Everything's been moved back to Ann's place. The landlady told me.
JIM. She's gotten rid of my students—I have no place to go ——
DOWNS. She's made you completely dependent on her, Jim. That's what she set out to do, and that's what she's achieved.
JIM. Why, for God's sake? What does she want of me?
DOWNS. She loves you, Jim. She wants you back. She told the doctor that. I won't try to explain it. I think there's something distorted in taking advantage of your being here to get you back this way. But I don't question that she loves you—and my advice to you is to be in love with her. That's the only way you'll get out of here quickly.
JIM. (*Quickly.*) I can't do it, Harry.
DOWNS. You lived with her for nine years—it can't be that difficult.
JIM. You don't know.
DOWNS. Ann is the only one who can help you, Jim.
JIM. (*His whole being protesting.*) I can't keep walking out on myself like that ——
DOWNS. Well, any other way will mean months—not in this place, because they can't keep you here. There's some kind of law, I was told, about a city hospital. You *can* be sent away to a State hospital—if that's what she wants.
JIM. Harry—I'm afraid of *this* place—when I think of an insane asylum ——
DOWNS. State hospital.
JIM. State hospital, I know. Forgive me, I don't care for the euphemism.
DOWNS. (*The briefest pause.*) Is there a euphemism for your life with Ann? (JIM *looks at* DOWNS.) That's the choice—the only choice.
JIM. (*Long pause.*) I don't know if she'll believe me now.
DOWNS. She *wants* to believe you.
JIM. God—just to get out of here, I'd ——
DOWNS. (*Rises from table.*) Now, don't get any notions that'll make trouble for you. You won't be a free man when you get out. You'll be released in her custody—that's one thing.
JIM. But after a while—when I'm out ——?

DOWNS. There's no "after a while" for you, Jim. You're trapped. I won't be able to help you, Jim—no one will. (*Takes step to* R., *turning away from* JIM.) It's a terrible thing to say—but no one can walk into that record office and make your name disappear. (*Turns back to* JIM.) That's how it is—people on the outside are more scared of someone who's been in a mental hospital than they are of one who's been to jail. You'll not only be living with Ann—you'll be living with the fear of exposure. It's a tough decision to make, Jim. Telling the truth has gotten you nowhere. (*Distinctly, making each word count.*) You're going to have to play ball—tell them the things they want to hear. (*The look* JIM *gives him suddenly makes* DOWNS *feel the guilt of his own years of compromise. He turns away.*) I know it goes against the grain. Certainly—no man is better for selling himself, believe me—and *you're* likely to suffer more than most. (*Turns back to* JIM: *there is no other way.*) Jim—you want to get out! (JIM *nods his head slowly.*)

## LIGHTS FADE QUICKLY

## ACT III

### SCENE 2

SCENE: *The same.*

TIME: *Four days later, Monday.*

BELLMAN *is sitting on down-stage end of table No. 2.* BARROW *is standing in front of table No. 3.* MISS WINGATE *is standing a step down-stage of* BARROW, *and to her R.* GREGORY *stands* L. *of* BARROW.

MISS WINGATE. (*To* BARROW.) Last Friday he played some Ping Pong.
GREGORY. (*Also, to* BARROW.) That was the first time since he came to One.
BARROW. (*To* WINGATE.) Was this voluntary, or did he have to be urged?
MISS WINGATE. He asked someone to play with him, as I remember. (*Looks to* GREGORY *for confirmation.*)
GREGORY. That's right.
BARROW. (*To* GREGORY.) Has he been eating?
GREGORY. Much better, the last few days.

71

MISS WINGATE. And Saturday he went to the movie we had in the auditorium.
BELLMAN. Would you say he's adjusted to hospital routine?
GREGORY. I think so.
BELLMAN. Does he speak of his wife?
GREGORY. Yes—some.
BELLMAN. Would you get him for me, Mr. Gregory? (GREGORY *leaves* R.)
MISS WINGATE. Mr. Downs reads a great deal. I thought of asking him to prepare a quiz show. (*Turns to* BELLMAN.) The men get pretty tired of the games we have here.
BARROW. (*A step down-stage, looks at* BELLMAN.) I know.
BELLMAN. (*As he gets up from table, crosses up-stage,* R. *of table No. 2, and comes to back of table No. 3.*) There isn't anything we can do.
MISS WINGATE. (*To* BELLMAN—*as he goes.*) Would you approve of the quiz show idea?
BELLMAN. We'll think about it, Miss Wingate. (JIM *enters from* R. *to approximately in front of table No. 1.*)
MISS WINGATE. (*Looks at* BARROW.) Yes, Doctor.
BARROW. (*A step down-stage when she sees* JIM.) Hello, Jim. May we see you, please?
BELLMAN. (*Turns.*) Hello, Mr. Downs. (MISS WINGATE *crosses* R., *in front of* JIM, *exits down* R.)
BARROW. How do you like it down here?
JIM. (*Tentatively.*) All right.
BARROW. You *look* much better than you did upstairs.
JIM. I was in quite a state up there, I guess.
BARROW. I would say so, Jim. Shall we sit down? (*They go to table No. 2.* JIM *sits chair down-stage end, on* R. BARROW *sits chair* L. BELLMAN *sits on up-stage end of table No. 2.* BARROW *arranges her papers.*) You won't mind if we give you a little test?
JIM. (*Frightened, but trying not to show it.*) Not at all. (*Turns to look at* BELLMAN, *who regards him impassively.*)
BARROW. This is a word-association test. I will give you a word from this list and I want you to answer with the first word that comes into your mind. For example, if I say "apple"—you may say "fruit" or "red" or "orange" or anything that occurs to you, but don't take time to think about it. The first word that occurs to you—remember. (*Sets her stop watch.*) All right. Black.
JIM. White. (BARROW *notes word and time taken.*)
BARROW. Street.

JIM. Car.
BARROW. Suicide.
JIM. (*A momentary catch.*) Death.
BARROW. Bed.
JIM. Soft.
BARROW. Friend.
JIM. Good.
BARROW. Trouble.
JIM. (*Brief pause. Repeats word as he thinks about it.*) Trouble—trouble.
BARROW. (*Looks up.*) Are you repeating the word?
JIM. I guess so. Trouble is trouble. I can't think of anything else.
BARROW. All right. (*Back to test.*) Mother.
JIM. Father.
BARROW. Murder.
JIM. Bad.
BARROW. Marriage.
JIM. Love.
BARROW. Wife. (JIM *looks at* BARROW *briefly—he is wrestling with himself. She repeats word.*) Wife.
JIM. (*Quietly.*) Sweetheart.
BELLMAN. (*Also, quietly.*) Just a minute, Mr. Downs. Dr. Barrow asked you to respond immediately, didn't she?
JIM. Yes—I ——
BELLMAN. In her instructions she said "Don't take time to think of an answer—we want the first word that occurs to you"—isn't that right?
JIM. Yes.
BELLMAN. In the light of what we know about your relationship with your wife—would you say that "sweetheart" represented an instinctive response?
JIM. Well ——
BARROW. We are trying to help you, Jim. You don't have to lie to us.
JIM. (*Strongly, recognizing trap he's in.*) I'm not lying—I ——
BELLMAN. (*Firmer now, he crosses back of table No. 1, comes downstage to front of table, to* R. *of* JIM.) There must have been some reason for your answer—you are obviously trying to mislead us.
JIM. (*Turns to* BELLMAN.) No—I'm not. Why should I?
BELLMAN. If Dr. Barrow had said "Charlotte," we might have expected such an answer.

JIM. (*Fighting for his life.*) No, Doctor—honestly—that isn't true any more.
BELLMAN. Can you really tell what *is* true at this point?
JIM. I think so—I——
BELLMAN. Either you were lying before—or you are lying now.
BARROW. (*Sympathetically.*) The discrepancy is too obvious, Jim—you can see that.
JIM. (*Forcefully.*) Isn't it *possible* to realize I've made a mistake?
BELLMAN. But this represents ——
BARROW. Of course it's possible. } *Together.*
JIM. (*Desperately—to* BARROW.) I was in love with my wife when I married her.
BARROW. You don't have to defend yourself, Jim. We are not asking you to be in love with her. If your feelings have ——
JIM. (*Protesting.*) But I am—I am—I *am* in love with her.
BELLMAN. And the quarrels and bickering ——?
JIM. That can happen to anybody. I lived with her, didn't I? We had years together ——
BELLMAN. (*As he crosses back of* JIM'S *chair, between tables* No. 1 *and* No. 2 *to back of table* No. 2.) The things you told Dr. Schlesinger ——
JIM. I was bitter. I was resentful—I had taken my life—I was mad at everybody. I must have said the things that gave only one side of the picture.
BELLMAN. (*Turns to* JIM.) You realize this change is rather sudden.
JIM. (*Now angry, he is slightly more controlled.*) I don't know about that. I don't know what constitutes sudden change. (*More deliberate.*) But I've been in the hospital more than two weeks, and I've had time to think. I've been away from both Ann *and* Charlotte—and I have a perspective I didn't have before.
BELLMAN. And what do you think now?
JIM. (*Controlled, he is more careful.*) I think of the *good* things I had with Ann. When we were living together I—I—I must have magnified the irritations and—made them important.
BELLMAN. And Charlotte?
JIM. (*A pause—quietly.*) I—I indulged myself, I guess —I —— (*Stops.*)
BELLMAN. (*A pause.*) What were you going to say?
JIM. I was going to say that most men do, at some time or other, but I realize I have no right to say that.
BELLMAN. Why?

JIM. Because I don't know, for one thing—and even if it were true—that's no excuse for me.
BELLMAN. I see. (*Pause.*) Do you want to go on with the test, Dr. Barrow?
BARROW. I think that's enough for now.
BELLMAN. All right, Mr. Downs, you may go. (JIM *gets up silently, leaves down* R. BELLMAN *crosses downstage between tables No. 1 and No. 2, looking after* JIM, *as he goes.*)
BARROW. (*Waits until* JIM *has gone, looks at* BELLMAN—*then, slowly.*) I am inclined to believe him.
BELLMAN. (*Turns to* BARROW.) We'll wait and see.—Let's check the test. (*Sits in* JIM'S *chair,* R. *of table No. 2.*)

## LIGHTS FADE QUICKLY

## ACT III

### SCENE 3

SCENE: *The same.*

TIME: *Three days later, Thursday. Visiting day.*

*Some visitors have already arrived and are sitting with patients at tables. All patients expecting visitors are standing in a group at* R. *Even patients not expecting anyone are in the group, getting a vicarious joy out of seeing others embrace, laugh, and cry. In group standing down* R. *are* JIM, CARLISLE, TAGER, *and* SCHLOSS, *and three or four extras.*

ANKORITIS *is being visited by his wife. They are seated at upstage end of table No. 2 when scene starts,* ANKORITIS *on* R., *his wife on* L. MAJOR *also has a female visitor, and they, too, are already seated, at up-stage end of table No. 3. The conversations between* ANKORITIS *and his wife, and between* MAJOR *and his visitor, should only be pantomimed, not heard.*

*When lights come up,* ANN *and her brother,* TOM, *have already been admitted. They stand* D. L., *near door.*

GREGORY. (*Examining* ANN'S *package—looks at* TOM—*then turns to* JIM, *calls.*) Downs. (ANN *and* TOM *cross to* C. GREGORY *sits, back of* HAN-

SEN'S *desk. He reads magazine through balance of scene.*)

JIM. (*Leaves group at same time, meets them* C.) Ann! I've been waiting. (*Shakes hands with* TOM.) Hello, Tom. It's nice of you to come.

TOM. (*Tall, heavy-set, much older than* ANN, *smiles as he takes* JIM'S *hand.*) You look fine, Jim.

JIM. I feel wonderful—better than in months.

ANN. Dr. Bellman was telling me this morning that you'd improved a great deal.

JIM. Let's sit down. (*As they go to front of table No. 3.*) What did you bring, Ann?

ANN. (*Gives him bag.*) Some fruit—candy.

JIM. (*To* TOM, *quietly, simply.*) You have no idea what her being here every visiting day has meant to me. (ANN *smiles. They sit,* JIM R. *of table No. 3, down-stage end,* ANN L. TOM *takes chair from* R. *of table No. 4, sits* L. *of* ANN.) She's been wonderful, Tom—simply wonderful. The whole hospital knows about her.

ANN. (*Laughing.*) Oh, Jim ——

JIM. It's true. Down here —— (*Turns to group* R.) You see those fellows standing over there? Well, sometimes they just stand there—even though no one ever comes to see them. I suppose, vicariously, they are visiting with everyone who comes in. After I leave you, Ann, each time—one or another of them has come to me and said, "You have a fine wife—I can tell." (ANN *laughs.*) Seriously.

ANN. Thank you, Jim. It's very nice of you to say that.

JIM. (*Simply, earnestly—with effort to make* ANN *believe him.*) Ann—we've wasted a lot of time on misunderstandings ——

ANN. Yes, Jim.

JIM. We'll make it up, Ann—you'll see.

ANN. If only I could believe you, Jim. This is the first time since you've been in the hospital you've spoken like this.

JIM. Ann, I ——

ANN. You were so impatient with me. Of course I realize what you were going through.

JIM. I'm sorry, Ann. It took time. Even after I got down here, I wasn't over the drug yet. I said a lot of things I really didn't mean—and I'm sorry. Ann, we're in love—we've always been in love—you know that.

ANN. I know I've always loved you, Jim.

JIM. I know.

ANN. Jim ——

JIM. Wait, let me finish. Being here was quite a shock—the whole experience was a shock. I've had time for lots of thinking—and one thing's become clear to me. I have a different sense of values from what I had before. For one thing, I don't have the unrealistic ambitions I had before. If I can settle down to a good job, that's all I want.

ANN. But——

JIM. I know what you're thinking. Look, Ann, if I have to, I'd even give up the theater.

ANN. Let's hope you don't have to do that.

JIM. But I would.

ANN. (*Brief pause—she wants to believe him.*) You do mean this, Jim—don't you?

JIM. Yes, I do.

ANN. (*Pause.*) I had a long talk with Dr. Bellman this morning.

JIM. (*Controlling his anxiety.*) What'd he say?

ANN. He's been getting fine reports about you. He said it may only be a few more days now.

JIM. He did?

ANN. (*Quickly.*) Now you mustn't get impatient. But he did say you were better.

TOM. Since it may only be a few days before you're discharged ——

ANN. Tom, really, I ——

TOM. (*His manner is quiet, controlled, he never raises his voice.*) Now let me take care of this, Ann. Ann didn't want me to come along, but I insisted. Now I don't want you to feel that because I'm Ann's brother I'm taking her side. I like you, Jim—I always have, and that's got nothing to do with Ann.

JIM. (*Apprehensive.*) What is it, Tom?

TOM. Well, now wait—I'll get to it. I just want to say that Ann didn't get her big brother to come down here to—er—put a whip to you—you know what I mean—eh—so eh—well, what it is—is just that Ann's friends and her doctor don't think it would be smart for Ann to take you back.

JIM. (*In desperate panic—he can hardly speak. He sees the trap closing, all his efforts in vain.*) Why not?

TOM. After all, you left her—you've been carrying on with another girl—you even tried to reach her here in the hospital.

JIM. But that's all over. I don't want to see this girl again.

TOM. Well, that's what we want to find out, Jim. If you're on the level about not wanting to see this girl again, then I think you ought to write her a letter and say so very plainly.

JIM. All right.
TOM. Or—if you prefer—if you want to see this girl and tell her how you feel—then I'll go with you.
JIM. (Barely audible.) Sure.
TOM. Ann has taken a terrible beating, Jim. All her friends—and, I must say, I agree with them—feel that she mustn't be hurt again. So—now that you may be getting out, this is what I want to say. You don't have to feel any obligation to Ann because of what she did for you in the hospital. Ann would have done that anyway, because she loves you. And you don't have to say now what you want to do—there's no pressure—no obligation. If you want to think about it—take your time. Only, once you give your word—that has to be *it*.
JIM. Of course.
ANN. (*To* JIM.) Please think it over, darling. I don't want you to make a mistake.
JIM. I know, dear. I—think it's very fair of Tom to put it this way.
TOM. You're a free man, Jim. Now take your time ——
JIM. Ann—what can I say? (*He can hardly breathe.*) I—I know we're in love. You certainly have been more decent than I deserve ——
ANN. Not at all, dear.
JIM. I said I was finished with—with Charlotte. I meant it. If—you'll have me back—I *want* to *go* back. I'm sure things will be better between us than they were.
ANN. They will, darling—I know they will.
JIM. I've been through quite an experience, Ann—you know that, better than anyone. I'm not over it yet—and—I'm still in this place. You'll have to give me time, Ann. After all, I—I've been reclaimed, so to speak.
ANN. It's been difficult, I know. (BELLMAN *enters* D. R. *He passes through group at* R., *on his way to speak to* ANKORITIS.)
BELLMAN. (*As he reaches table No. 2, he sees* ANN.) Hello, Mrs. Downs.
ANN. (*Looks up.*) How do you do, Dr. Bellman? (BELLMAN *goes to* ANKORITIS—*speaks with him and his wife.*)
JIM. (*Rises.*) I'm tired, Ann. Will you forgive me?
ANN. (*Rises.*) Certainly.
TOM. (*Rises.*) And we'll take care of that other matter when you get out.
JIM. Sure. It was good to see you, Tom. (*To* ANN.) Bye, darling. (*Smiles, not sure whether to embrace her or not. Takes a step to her, she to him. Slowly, tentatively, their arms go out, and they embrace.*

*Then he takes package* ANN *brought him, smiles to her again, turns, and slowly goes off* D. R.)
CARLISLE. (*When* JIM *reaches group as he goes off.*) She never misses coming to see you on a visiting day. (*Pats* JIM's *shoulder as he goes by.*)
ANN. (*Has watched* JIM *go off, then turns to* TOM.) Wait for me. I want to speak to Bellman a minute. (*Crosses a few steps to near table No. 2.*) Dr. Bellman?
BELLMAN. (*To* ANKORITIS.) Excuse me. (*Steps down to* ANN, *with a bright smile.*) How are you, Mrs. Downs?
ANN. I'm fine, thank you, Doctor. I agree with you—there's a tremendous improvement in Jim.
BELLMAN. Do you think he's telling the truth now?
ANN. I'm sure of it.
BELLMAN. Well—we'll see. How do you feel about taking him back?
ANN. I love him, Doctor.
BELLMAN. And this other girl?
ANN. That's finished.
BELLMAN. I'll have another talk with him myself tomorrow. It may only be another day.
ANN. Thank you, Doctor. (BELLMAN *nods, returns to* ANKORITIS. ANN *goes to* TOM. *He helps her on with her coat.*)

## LIGHTS FADE QUICKLY

## ACT III

### SCENE 4

SCENE: *The same.*

TIME: *The next day, Friday.*

BELLMAN *and* JIM *are seated at table No. 3.* BELLMAN L., JIM R.

*The interview is already in progress.*

BELLMAN. Then you think you feel differently now from when you came here?
JIM. Yes, I do.
BELLMAN. In what way do you feel differently?

JIM. I suppose in the matter of learning about myself. I don't think I have the unrealistic ambitions I had before.
BELLMAN. What do you mean by that?
JIM. Well, after a certain number of years in a profession without making the grade, I'd say it was realistic to think in terms of other work.
BELLMAN. What do you plan to do if you leave here?
JIM. Go home.
BELLMAN. (*A brief pause.*) Is that all?
JIM. Well—I'd need time to recover——
BELLMAN. Recover from what?
JIM. From this whole experience.
BELLMAN. Then you don't *really* think you're well yet?
JIM. Yes, I do——
BELLMAN. Then why did you say "recover"?
JIM. I meant——
BELLMAN. What?
JIM. Well, I have no job—it will take time to find something.
BELLMAN. "Recover" doesn't mean finding a job.
JIM. I *know* that. I simply used the word to——
BELLMAN. How?
JIM. In the sense of getting back to normal.
BELLMAN. And what do you mean by normal?
JIM. Well, living here is——
BELLMAN. Yes?
JIM. (*A pause, catching himself.*) By normal I only meant working again—living at home—being back with my wife.
BELLMAN. Then you don't really *have* a plan for your future?
JIM. Well—I could start by going back to my teaching.
BELLMAN. Are you a good teacher?
JIM. I think so.
BELLMAN. Can you make a living by your teaching?
JIM. Fair.
BELLMAN. Enough to support you and your wife?
JIM. If we're careful. I'll have to find more regular work, of course.
BELLMAN. What kind of work?
JIM. I don't know at the moment, Doctor—I—I'm not unintelligent—I'm sure there's something I can do.
BELLMAN. I see. Do you feel you will need psychiatric help when you leave here?

JIM. Do *you* think I will?
BELLMAN. I'm asking you.
JIM. I just don't know, Doctor.
BELLMAN. Do you feel you're cured?
JIM. I think so.
BELLMAN. Then you *don't* think you will need help on the outside?
JIM. No. I don't.
BELLMAN. One more thing. Do you feel that having been here will affect your future?
JIM. How do you mean?
BELLMAN. How would you react if the people you worked with knew you had been in a mental hospital?
JIM. If they know—they know. There's nothing I can do about it.
BELLMAN. But how would you feel?
JIM. I'd expect them to think of me in the light of the present. If my work is satisfactory I can only hope the past will play no part in their judgment.
BELLMAN. I see. And you feel now you're ready to go home?
JIM. Yes.
BELLMAN. When do you think you should leave?
JIM. That's up to you, Doctor.
BELLMAN. (*A brief pause.*) That's all for now.
JIM. (*Gets up, starts off R., stops, turns slowly to* BELLMAN.) Is it unreasonable to ask how long it will be?
BELLMAN. (*Slowly.*) No.
JIM. (*His throat is dry.*) Then may I know?
BELLMAN. (*Looks at* JIM *carefully—looks back at chart, which is on table, in front of him, then, to* JIM, *after a long pause.*) Call your wife.
JIM. (*Unable to believe.*) What?
BELLMAN. Call your wife. You may go home today.
JIM. (*Simply.*) Thank you, Doctor. (*Takes a few steps back, to* L.) May I call from here? (*Indicates with his head the phone on* HANSEN'S *desk.*)
BELLMAN. (*Turns to look at phone, then back to* JIM.) Yes. You may use that phone. (JIM *crosses* L. *to phone.* BELLMAN *closes chart, rises, turns to* JIM.) You'll be in her custody, you understand.
JIM. (*Quickly.*) Yes, sir. (BELLMAN *turns, goes off* D. R. JIM *slowly dials number, and waits.*) Ann? I'm discharged. I can leave today. Dr. Bellman just said so. Ann, would you bring a tie for me—and my overcoat? Thank you, dear. (*He can scarcely control his tears.*) You won't

be long—will you? (*He almost falls over phone as he replaces the receiver. The tears now come without inhibition. Slowly, he makes his way off stage,* D. R., *sobbing audibly, but still quietly—making no effort whatever to hide his face, knowing in his heart he has simply exchanged one evil for another.*)

## CURTAIN

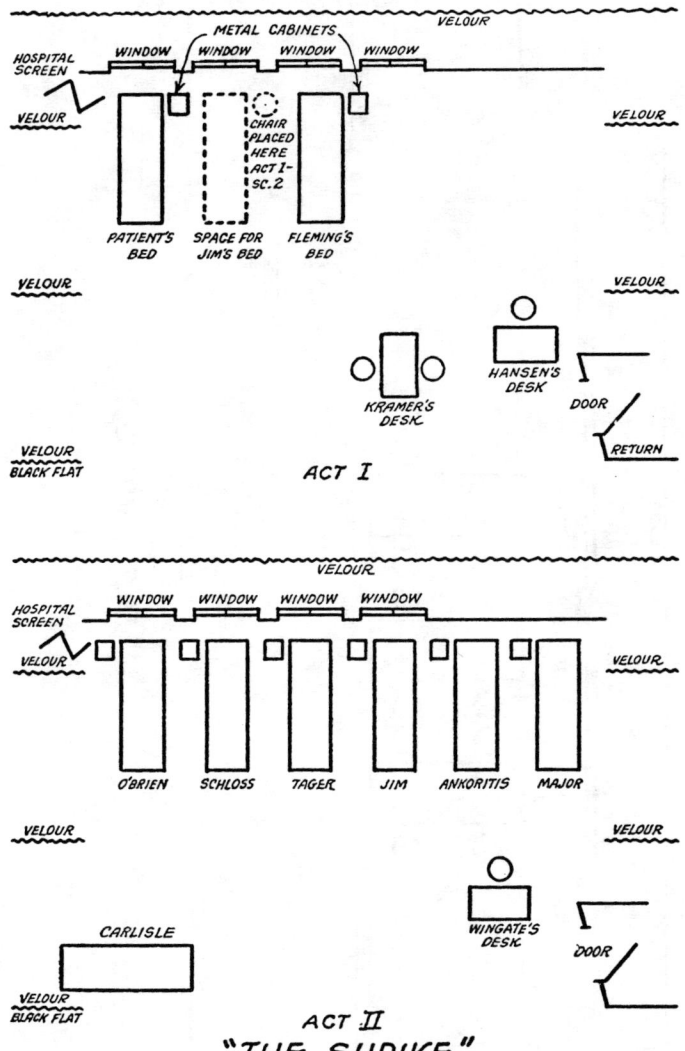

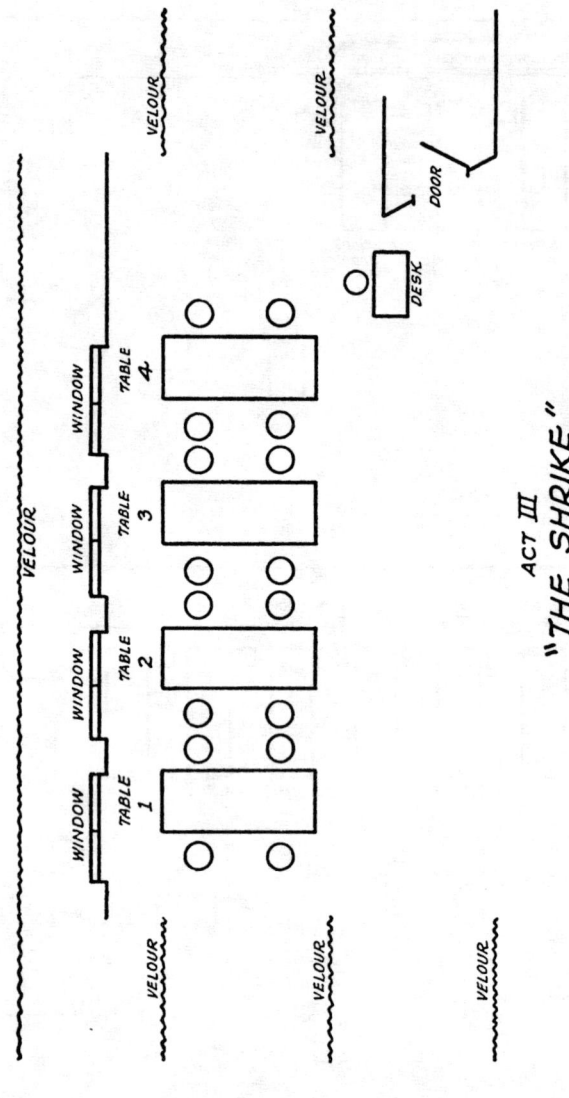

# PROP LIST

## Act I—Scene 1

(2) Beds (Sheets, pillows, blanket, charts foot of bed)
(2) Cabinets and lamps—Jim's practical
(1) Chair R. of Fleming's cabinet
Matches, cigarettes, $1 bill Fleming's cabinet drawer
Desk table D. L. C.—telephone, ashtray, blood pressure gauge, medical journal, pen stethoscope, Schlesinger chart D. S. R., 2 chairs L. and R.—L. chair, angled (close)
(1) Table D. L.—lamp, practical, phone (dial), pencil, charts, pen, telegram (cover), pad and pencil in drawer, 1 chair above table
Bed screen U. R.
Doorbell, phone bell off L.
Check wagon entrance

## Act I—Scene 2

Chart for Jim's bed
Strike screen off R.

Slippers for Jim's bed R. C.

## Act I—Scene 3

Screen U. R.
Pencilled letter and envelope for Jim
Chair L.—head of Jim's bed place
Strike saline stand
Chair R. of Kramer's desk pushes under table

Strike coffee
Chair L. Kramer's desk, angled (midway)
Strike Ann's bag off L.

## Act I—Scene 4

Table L. C. and 2 chairs, move C., front L.
Chairs L. and R. of table, R. angled

Screen moves C.
Fix Jim's bed

## Act I—Scene 5

C. table and 2 chairs, move to L. C., front R., R. chair under table, L. angled

Screen moves U. R., angled off R.

### Act II—Scene 1

7 beds (mattress, blanket, sheets, pillows—except Jim's which has 2 soiled sheets, 1 blanket—no charts)
5 metal bedside cabinets
Cigarettes and matches No. 1 bed
N. Y. Times No. 2 bed
Cards No. 4 bed
Pencil, sketchbook, sketches, No. 6 bed

Rollers No. 6 bed
Dixie cups, water, L. cabinet
Bed No. 5, cover pillow—lamps bent down
Carlisle's bed—head on stage
D. L. desk—phone, clipboard, pen and pencil, chair above pushed under
Screen U. R.

### Act II—Scene 2

Table C., chart, 2 chairs above and R. chair angled front U. S.

Screen moves C.

### Act II—Scene 3

Strike C. table and 2 chairs

Move screen U. R.

### Act II—Scene 4

Remake O'Brien's bed
Strike O'Brien's shoes

Clear D. L. desk except phone

### Act II—Scene 5

Checkerboard foot bed No. 2
Cribbage board, magazine, foot bed No. 4

Desk L. angled, props struck—2 chairs above and D. L. of desk
Clear Ann's package

### Act III—Scene 1

4 tables
16 chairs

Desk L.—phone—Mouthpiece L.—chair above

### Act III—Scene 2

Clear Ann's package

Straighten chairs, table No. 3

### Act III—Scene 3

Straighten chairs, table No. 2

### Act III—Scene 4

Tom's chair replaced

# TODAY'S HOTTEST NEW PLAYS

☐ **MOLLY SWEENEY by Brian Friel, Tony Award-Winning Author of *Dancing at Lughnasa*.** Told in the form of monologues by three related characters, *Molly Sweeney* is mellifluous, Irish storytelling at its dramatic best. Blind since birth, Molly recounts the effects of an eye operation that was intended to restore her sight but which has unexpected and tragic consequences. *"Brian Friel has been recognized as Ireland's greatest living playwright. Molly Sweeney confirms that Mr. Friel still writes like a dream. Rich with rapturous poetry and the music of rising and falling emotions...Rarely has Mr. Friel written with such intoxicating specificity about scents, colors and contours." - New York Times.* [2M, 1W]

☐ **SWINGING ON A STAR (The Johnny Burke Musical) by Michael Leeds. 1996 Tony Award Nominee for Best Musical.** The fabulous songs of Johnny Burke are perfectly represented here in a series of scenes jumping from a 1920s Chicago speakeasy to a World War II USO Show and on through the romantic high jinks of the Bob Hope/Bing Crosby "Road Movies." Musical numbers include such favorites as "Pennies from Heaven," "Misty," "Ain't It a Shame About Mame," "Like Someone in Love," and, of course, the Academy Award winning title song, "Swinging on a Star." *"A WINNER. YOU'LL HAVE A BALL!" - New York Post. "A dazzling, toe-tapping, finger-snapping delight!" - ABC Radio Network. "Johnny Burke wrote his songs with moonbeams!" - New York Times.* [3M, 4W]

☐ **THE MONOGAMIST by Christopher Kyle.** Infidelity and mid-life anxiety force a forty-something poet to reevaluate his 60s values in a late 80s world. *"THE BEST COMEDY OF THE SEASON. Trenchant, dark and jagged. Newcomer Christopher Kyle is a playwright whose social satire comes with a nasty, ripping edge - Molière by way of Joe Orton." - Variety. "By far the most stimulating playwright I've encountered in many a buffaloed moon." - New York Magazine. "Smart, funny, articulate and wisely touched with rue...the script radiates a bright, bold energy." - The Village Voice.* [2M, 3W]

☐ **DURANG/DURANG by Christopher Durang.** These cutting parodies of *The Glass Menagerie* and *A Lie of the Mind*, along with the other short plays in the collection, prove once and for all that Christopher Durang is our theater's unequivocal master of outrageous comedy. *"The fine art of parody has returned to theater in a production you can sink your teeth and mind into, while also laughing like an idiot." - New York Times. "If you need a break from serious drama, the place to go is Christopher Durang's silly, funny, over-the-top sketches." - TheatreWeek.* [3M, 4W, flexible casting]

**DRAMATISTS PLAY SERVICE, INC.**
440 Park Avenue South, New York, New York 10016   212-683-8960   Fax 212-213-1539

## TODAY'S HOTTEST NEW PLAYS

❏ **THREE VIEWINGS by Jeffrey Hatcher.** Three comic-dramatic monologues, set in a midwestern funeral parlor, interweave as they explore the ways we grieve, remember, and move on. *"Finally, what we have been waiting for: a new, true, idiosyncratic voice in the theater. And don't tell me you hate monologues; you can't hate them more than I do. But these are much more: windows into the deep of each speaker's fascinating, paradoxical, unique soul, and windows out into a gallery of surrounding people, into hilarious and horrific coincidences and conjunctions, into the whole dirty but irresistible business of living in this damnable but spellbinding place we presume to call the world."* - New York Magazine. [1M, 2W]

❏ **HAVING OUR SAY by Emily Mann.** The Delany Sisters' Bestselling Memoir is now one of Broadway's Best-Loved Plays! Having lived over one hundred years apiece, Bessie and Sadie Delany have plenty to say, and their story is not simply African-American history or women's history...it is our history as a nation. *"The most provocative and entertaining family play to reach Broadway in a long time."* - New York Times. *"Fascinating, marvelous, moving and forceful."* - Associated Press. [2W]

❏ **THE YOUNG MAN FROM ATLANTA Winner of the 1995 Pulitzer Prize. by Horton Foote.** An older couple attempts to recover from the suicide death of their only son, but the menacing truth of why he died, and what a certain Young Man from Atlanta had to do with it, keeps them from the peace they so desperately need. *"Foote ladles on character and period nuances with a density unparalleled in any living playwright."* - NY Newsday. [5M, 4W]

❏ **SIMPATICO by Sam Shepard.** Years ago, two men organized a horse racing scam. Now, years later, the plot backfires against the ringleader when his partner decides to come out of hiding. *"Mr. Shepard writing at his distinctive, savage best."* - New York Times. [3M, 3W]

❏ **MOONLIGHT by Harold Pinter.** The love-hate relationship between a dying man and his family is the subject of Harold Pinter's first full-length play since *Betrayal*. *"Pinter works the language as a master pianist works the keyboard."* - New York Post. [4M, 2W, 1G]

❏ **SYLVIA by A.R. Gurney.** This romantic comedy, the funniest to come along in years, tells the story of a twenty-two year old marriage on the rocks, and of Sylvia, the dog who turns it all around. *"A delicious and dizzy new comedy."* - New York Times. *"FETCHING! I hope it runs longer than Cats!"* - New York Daily News. [2M, 2W]

**DRAMATISTS PLAY SERVICE, INC.**
440 Park Avenue South, New York, New York 10016  212-683-8960  Fax 212-213-1539